AF706086

A COMPARATIVE STUDY OF THE MONEY LAUNDERING Laws/Regulations in Nigeria, the United States and the United Kingdom

EHI ERIC ESOIMEME

ERIC PRESS

© Ehi Eric Esoimeme 2014

All rights reserved. No part of this publication may be reproduced, stored in a retrieval system, or transmitted in any form or by any means, electronic, mechanical, photocopying, recording, or otherwise without the prior permission of the author.

ISBN-10: 978-2787-90-6
ISBN-13: 978-978-2787-90-3
Published by Eric Press
Manufactured in the United States of America

Acknowledgements

I take this opportunity to express my deep sense of gratitude to Mr Ian Ross for the foreword to this book that he has kindly written.

I express my sincere appreciation to my mother, Dr Angela Esoimeme, for her unwavering support, encouragement and supreme patience. I consider myself particularly fortunate to have her as my mother. She created an environment of homely peace and tranquillity while I strove to ensure that this publication was of unequalled excellence.

TABLE OF CONTENTS

FOREWORD ..... **xiii**

PREFACE ..... **xv**

TABLE OF CASES ..... **xix**

TABLES OF LEGISLATION ..... **xxi**

TABLE OF INTERNATIONAL CONVENTIONS ..... **xxv**

LIST OF ABBREVIATIONS ..... **xxvii**

CHAPTER 1
INTRODUCTION TO MONEY LAUNDERING AND TERRORIST FINANCING **1**

1.1 WHAT IS MONEY LAUNDERING? 1

1.2 STAGES OF MONEY LAUNDERING 2

1.2.1 PLACEMENT 3

1.2.2 LAYERING 3

1.2.3 INTEGRATION 4

1.3 TERRORIST FINANCING 4

1.4 ANTI-MONEY LAUNDERING RISK ASSESSMENT 6

1.4.1 IDENTIFICATION OF SPECIFIC RISK CATEGORIES 6

1.4.1.1 Products And Services 7

1.4.1.2 Customers And Entities 7

1.4.1.3 Geographic Locations 8

1.4.2 ANALYSIS OF SPECIFIC RISK CATEGORIES 9

1.4.3 DEVELOPING THE BANK'S AML COMPLIANCE PROGRAMME BASED UPON ITS RISK ASSESSMENT 10

1.4.3.1 Customer Due Diligence 11

1.4.3.2 Enhanced Due Diligence 12

1.4.3.3 Senior Management Approval 14
1.4.3.4 Enhanced Ongoing Monitoring 14
1.4.4 IMPLICATIONS OF FAILURE OF A FIRM TO CONDUCT ENHANCED DUE DILIGENCE (EDD) AND ENHANCED ONGOING MONITORING (EOM) 15
1.5 INTERNATIONAL BODIES/ORGANISATIONS 16
1.5.1 FINANCIAL ACTION TASK FORCE 16
1.5.2 BASEL COMMITTEE 17
1.5.3 THE WOLFSBERG GROUP OF INTERNATIONAL FINANCIAL INSTITUTIONS 18
1.5.4 INTERNATIONAL MONETARY FUND 20
1.5.5 THE WORLD BANK 23
1.5.6 THE INTERNATIONAL ORGANIZATION OF SECURITIES COMMISSION 24
1.5.7 INTERNATIONAL ASSOCIATION OF INSURANCE SUPERVISORS 25
1.5.8 TRANSPARENCY INTERNATIONAL 26

CHAPTER 2
REPORTING REQUIREMENTS 27
2.1 RELEVANT MONEY LAUNDERING LAWS/REGULATIONS 28
2.1.1 NIGERIA 28
2.1.2 UNITED STATES 28
2.1.3 UNITED KINGDOM 29
2.2 REPORTING REQUIREMENTS 29
2.2.1 NIGERIA 29
2.2.1.1 What To File 29
2.2.1.2 Where To File 30
2.2.1.3 When To File 31
2.2.1.4 Confidentiality Of STRs /Tipping Off (General Rule) 31
2.2.1.5 Confidentiality Of STRs/Tipping Off (Exception) 31
2.2.1.6 Penalties 32
2.2.2 UNITED STATES 32
2.2.2.1 What To File 32
2.2.2.1.1 Banks 32
2.2.2.1.2 Money Service Businesses 33

2.2.2.2 Where To File 35
2.2.2.2.1 Banks *35*
2.2.2.2.2 Money Service Businesses *35*
2.2.2.3 When To File 35
2.2.2.3.1 Banks *35*
2.2.2.3.2 Money Service Businesses *36*
2.2.2.4 Confidentiality Of SARs/Tipping Off (General Rule) 36
2.2.2.4.1 Banks And Money Service Businesses *36*
2.2.2.5 Confidentiality Of SARs/Tipping Off (Exceptions) 37
2.2.2.5.1 Banks And Money Service Businesses *37*
2.2.2.6 Penalties 38
2.2.2.6.1 Civil Penalty *38*
2.2.2.6.2 Criminal Penalty *39*
2.2.3 UNITED KINGDOM 39
2.2.3.1 What To File 39
2.2.3.2 Where To File 39
2.2.3.3 When To File 40
2.2.3.4 Confidentiality Of SARs/Tipping Off (General Rule) 40
2.2.3.5 Confidentiality Of SARs/Tipping Off (Exception) 40
2.2.3.6 Penalties 41
2.2.3.6.1 Tipping Off *41*
2.2.3.6.2 Failure To File A SAR *42*
2.3 DISCUSSION 42
2.3.1 WHAT TO FILE 42
2.3.2 WHEN A TRANSACTION REQUIRES REPORTING 44
2.3.3 CONFIDENTIALITY OF SARS 44
2.4 CONCLUSION 45

CHAPTER 3
MONEY LAUNDERING OFFENCE 47
3.1 THE CRIME OF MONEY LAUNDERING 48
3.1.1 NIGERIA 51
3.1.2 UNITED STATES 52
3.1.3 UNITED KINGDOM 55
3.2 PREDICATE OFFENCES FOR MONEY LAUNDERING (DOMESTIC CRIMES) 56

3.2.1 NIGERIA ... 57
3.2.2 UNITED STATES ... 57
3.2.3 UNITED KINGDOM ... 61
3.3 PREDICATE OFFENCES FOR MONEY LAUNDERING (FOREIGN CRIMES) ... 61
3.3.1 NIGERIA ... 61
3.3.2 UNITED STATES ... 62
3.3.3 UNITED KINGDOM ... 63
3.4 PENALTIES ... 64
3.4.1 NIGERIA ... 64
3.4.2 UNITED STATES ... 65
3.4.3 UNITED KINGDOM ... 65
3.5 DISCUSSION ... 65
3.5.1 PREDICATE OFFENCES FOR MONEY LAUNDERING (DOMESTIC CRIMES) ... 65
3.5.2 PREDICATE OFFENCES FOR MONEY LAUNDERING (FOREIGN CRIMES) ... 67
3.6 CONCLUSION ... 68

CHAPTER 4
POLITICALLY EXPOSED PERSONS ... 69
4.1 APPLICATION OF THE PEPs DEFINITION ... 70
4.1.1 NIGERIA ... 72
4.1.2 UNITED STATES ... 72
4.2 DISCUSSION ... 72
4.2.1 PROTECTING THE FINANCIAL SYSTEM AGAINST CORRUPT PEPS ... 73
4.2.2 UPHOLDING EQUALITY BEFORE THE LAW ... 74
4.2.2.1 Differential Treatment ... 74
4.2.2.2 Prohibited Grounds ... 75
4.2.2.3 Without Objective and Reasonable Justification ... 76
4.2.2.4 No Reasonable Relationship of Proportionality ... 76
4.3 CONCLUSION ... 77

CHAPTER 5
CASH COURIERS 79
5.1 DECLARATION SYSTEM 81
5.1.1 NIGERIA 81
5.1.1.1 Green Exit 81
5.1.1.2 Red Exit 81
5.1.2 UNITED STATES 82
5.1.3 UNITED KINGDOM 83
5.1.3.1 When to use the blue channel 83
5.1.3.2 When to use the green channel 83
5.1.3.3 When to use the red channel or red-point phone 83
5.2 DISCUSSION 84
5.2.1 PROTECTING THE FINANCIAL SYSTEM AGAINST MONEY LAUNDERERS AND TERRORISTS 84
5.2.2 UPHOLDING EQUALITY BEFORE THE LAW 85
5.2.2.1 Differential Treatment 86
5.2.2.2 Prohibited Grounds 87
5.2.2.3 Without Objective and Reasonable Justification 87
5.3 CONCLUSION 88

CHAPTER 6
COMPLIANCE OFFICERS 89
6.1 THE TITLE OF THE INDIVIDUAL RESPONSIBLE FOR ANTI MONEY LAUNDERING COMPLIANCE 90
6.1.1 NIGERIA 90
6.1.2 UNITED STATES 90
6.1.3 UNITED KINGDOM 91
6.2 DUTIES AND RESPONSIBLITIES 91
6.2.1 NIGERIA 91
6.2.2 UNITED STATES 91
6.2.3 UNITED KINGDOM 91
6.3 DISCUSSION 92
6.3.1 DUTIES AND RESPONSIBILITIES 92
6.4 CONCLUSION 93

CHAPTER 7

THE OFFENCE OF BRIBERY 95

7.1 RELEVANT BRIBERY LAWS AND REGULATIONS 96
7.1.1 UNITED KINGDOM 96
7.1.2 UNITED STATES 96
7.1.3 NIGERIA 96
7.2 STRICT LIABILITY 96
7.3 EXTRATERRITORIAL JURISDICTION 101
7.4 PENALTIES 106
7.5 CONCLUSION 107

CHAPTER 8

PLEA BARGAINING 109

8.1 DEFINITION OF PLEA BARGAINING 110
8.2 HISTORY OF PLEA BARGAINING 111
8.3 THE NATURE OF PLEA BARGAINING 112
8.4 DISCUSSION 112
8.4.1 NIGERIA 113
8.4.2 UNITED STATES 120
8.4.3 UNITED KINGDOM 126
8.5 CONCLUSION 128

CHAPTER 9

CUSTOMER DUE DILIGENCE 129

9.1 CUSTOMER INFORMATION REQUIRED 130
9.1.1 NIGERIA 130
9.1.2 UNITED STATES 132
9.1.3 UNITED KINGDOM 133
9.2 VERIFICATION THROUGH DOCUMENTS 134
9.2.1 NIGERIA 134
9.2.2 UNITED STATES 135
9.2.3 UNITED KINGDOM 135
9.3 VERIFICATION THROUGH NON-DOCUMENTARY METHODS 137

9.3.1 NIGERIA 137
9.3.2 UNITED STATES 137
9.3.3 UNITED KINGDOM 138
9.4 DISCUSSION 140
9.4.1 MEANING OF 'CUSTOMER' 140
9.4.2 DIRECT DISCRIMINATION 142
9.4.2.1 Differential Treatment 143
9.5 CONCLUSION 144

CHAPTER 10
RECORD KEEPING 145
10.1 THE RISK-BASED APPROACH TO RECORD-KEEPING REQUIREMENTS 146
10.2 CONCLUSION 147

CHAPTER 11
LEVEL OF COMPLIANCE 149
11.1 NIGERIA 149
11.2 UNITED STATES 150
11.3 UNITED KINGDOM 150
11.4 DISCUSSION 153
11.4.1 QUALIFICATION OF COMPLIANCE OFFICERS 153
11.5 CONCLUSION 154

APPENDIX 1
GLOSSARY OF TERMINOLOGY 155

APPENDIX 2
BIBLIOGRAPHY 161

INDEX 169

FOREWORD

Money laundering is said to be the nearest thing to 'financial alchemy'.

Hence, for me, it is not just a pleasure, but a highly stimulating experience to write the foreword for this excellent book.

Ehi Esoimeme engages with issues that many either oversimplify or avoid altogether. He admirably met the challenge of reconciling legal, jurisdictional and operational issues akin to money laundering. Of course, full or actual reconciliation is not always possible. Creating an understanding of the complexity of language to help 'finders of fact' register this as a genuine vocational and workable anti–money laundering commodity and professional resource was but one crucial challenge ably achieved. One cannot reduce issues of law and acquisitive financial crime to a state of simplicity that does not exist.

Equally, money laundering, being such an amorphous entity as a crime, is arguably de facto immeasurable in a full and real sense. Many texts address specific points of reference and requisite money laundering criminality, but here we see a splendidly holistic approach to presenting answers to the questions it poses.

Writing a widely acceptable book on the massive issue of money laundering and the fragmented state of the law across key jurisdictions—as in Nigeria, the United Kingdom and the United States of America—needs order and method, as well as a flexible and running thread to connect cohesion and meaning to it all. This book provides this.

The comparatives and overlaps are well presented and neatly contextualized to keep them proportionate. The highest quality grasp of legal theory resonates throughout. A dynamic and synergy in the linking chapters engages the reader in the style I have come to know from Ehi Esoimeme. Current challenges are clear, and future remedies and workable answers and methods and polices are explained or hinted at. The book encourages conceptual thought as well as finite and robust guidance for learning.

In essence, what we have in this superb text is clarity and not mere description of the challenges and issues it addresses.

Therefore you, as either a fellow professional or an infrequent but interested observer of money laundering, knowing what money laundering is, how it has advanced more than ever with new ways, what it causes and how we attempt to govern this massive spectre of crime legally and operationally, cannot help but benefit from this book—whatever your vocation or whatever part you have in combating it.

Ian Ross, MSc, CICA, IAiP

Head of Operations, Cyber and Financial Crime

Jasper Global Corporation (JGC)

PREFACE

The Financial Action Task Force (FATF Recommendations set out a comprehensive and consistent framework of measures that countries should implement in order to combat money laundering, terrorist financing and financing of the proliferation of weapons of mass destruction.

Although countries have followed the advice of the FATF by enacting laws that require financial institutions and designated nonfinancial businesses and professions (DNFBPs to implement certain measures that can combat money laundering and terrorist financing, the approaches adopted in these different countries are not identical.

This book compares the approaches adopted in Nigeria, the United States and the United Kingdom in relation to reporting requirements, money laundering offences, politically exposed persons, cash couriers, compliance officers, offences of bribery, confiscation measures, customer due-diligence measures, record keeping and level of compliance. The aim of this comparison is to determine what the best approach is—the one that strikes a fair balance between protecting the financial system against money launderers and upholding equality before the law.

This book relies mainly on primary and secondary data drawn from the public domain. It also relies on documentary research.

Chapter 1 introduces readers to what money laundering is. In addition to defining money laundering and highlighting the different international bodies charged with fighting it, the chapter breaks down the money laundering risk-assessment process in a way that anyone who is interested can understand.

Chapter 2 compares the reporting requirements in Nigeria with those of the United States and the United Kingdom to determine whether Nigeria needs to adopt the approach of these countries or if there is no need for reform. This comparison is done under five different subheadings: 'What to File', 'Where to File', 'When to File', 'Confidentiality of Suspicious Activity Reports' and 'Penalties'.

Chapter 3 compares the approaches in Nigeria, the United States and the United Kingdom as they relate to money laundering offences. The comparison is done under four subheadings: 'The Crime of Money Laundering', 'Predicate Offences for Money Laundering (Domestic Crimes)', 'Predicate Offences for Money Laundering (Foreign Crimes)' and 'Penalties'.

Chapter 4 compares the approaches in Nigeria, the United States and the United Kingdom as they relate to politically exposed persons (PEPs) under the subheading 'Application of the PEP Definition'.

Chapter 5 compares the approaches in Nigeria, the United States and the United Kingdom as they relate to cash couriers under the subheading 'Declaration System'.

Chapter 6 compares the approaches in Nigeria, the United States and the United Kingdom as they relate to compliance officers. The comparison is done under two subheadings: 'The Title of the Individual Responsible for Anti–Money Laundering Compliance' and 'Duties and Responsibilities'.

Chapter 7 compares the approaches in Nigeria, the United States and the United Kingdom as they relate to the predicate offence of bribery. The comparison is done under three subheadings: 'Strict Liability', 'Extraterritorial Jurisdiction' and 'Penalties'.

Chapter 8 compares the approaches in Nigeria, the United States and the United Kingdom as they relate to the application of the concept of plea bargaining.

Chapter 9 compares the approaches in Nigeria, the United States and the United Kingdom as they relate to customer due-diligence measures.

Chapter 10 is a critical analysis of the rule-based approach that is applied to record-keeping requirements. The analysis is done under the subheading 'The Risk-Based Approach to Record-Keeping Requirements'.

Chapter 11 determines the level of compliance with anti–money laundering measures in Nigeria, the United States and the United Kingdom.

This book is aimed at both undergraduate and postgraduate law students. It is also aimed at financial institutions and professionals in the field of anti–money laundering compliance.

Ehi Eric Esoimeme Esq., Llb (Unilag), Bl, Ica (Manchester), Llm (Cardiff), PhD (in View) (Unilag)

Managing Associate at Deji Sasegbon and Co.

Deputy Editor in Chief of Dsc Publications Ltd.

Editorial Board Member at the *International Journal of Law and Society*

Contributor at the *Journal of Money Laundering Control* (the world's only quarterly, peer-reviewed journal)

Contributor at the *Journal of Financial Crime*

Contributor at *Law Digest* (Africa's leading law journal)

Contributor at Kyc360 (the world's leading platform for anti-money laundering professionals)

Member of the Association of Certified Anti-Money Laundering Specialists (Acams)

Author of *Deterring and Detecting Money Laundering and Terrorist Financing*

Author of *The Risk-Based Approach to Combating Money Laundering and Terrorist Financing*

Author of *Banker-Customer Relationship: A Practical Legal Guide*

Author of approved scholarly papers (Ssrn) (Us)

Website: https://ehiericesoimeme.com/

TABLE OF CASES

REFERENCES ARE TO PARAGRAPH NUMBERS

NIGERIA

Federal Republic of Nigeria v. Cecilia Ibru	8.4.1
Federal Republic of Nigeria v. Alamieyeseigha	8.4.1
Federal Republic of Nigeria v. Tafa Balogun	8.4.1
Federal Republic of Nigeria v. Lucky Igbinedion	8.4.1

UNITED STATES

Lafler v. Fyre (March 2012)	8.4.2
Missouri v. Cooper (March 2012)	8.4.2
SEC v. Alcatel-Lucent, SA Case No 10 – Cv – 24620 (SD Fla Dec 27 2010) ECF No. 1	7.2
SEC v. ABB LTD, Case No 10, 10-cv-1648,(DDC Sep 29 2009) ECF No 1	7.2
SEC v. RAE Sys Inc Case No 10-Cv-2093 (DDC Dec 10 2010) ECF No 1	7.2
SEC v. ABB Ltd, Case No 4-cv-1141 (DDC July 6 2004) ECF No.1	7.2
SEC v. UTS Starcom Inc No 09-cv-6094 (ND Cal Dec 31 2009) ECF No 1	7.2
SEC v. Schering – Plough Corp No 4-cv-945 (DDC June 9 2004) ECF No 1	7.2
SEC v. Innospec Inc, No 10-cv-448 (DDC March 18 2010) ECF No 1	7.2
SEC v. Technip No 10-cv-2289. (SD Tex June 28 2010) ECF No 1	7.2

SEC v. Halliburton Company and KBR INC Civil Action 4:09 -399	7.2
SEC v. Magyar Telekom Plc and Deutsche Telekom AG Case No 11 – Cv -9646 (S.D.N.Y Dec 29 2011) ECF No 1	7.2
SEC v. ENI S.P.A and Snamprogetti Netherlands BV Case No 10-cv-2414	7.2
SEC v. Siemens Aktiengesellschaft, Case No 08-cv-2167 (DDC Dec 12 2008) ECF No 1	7.2
SEC v. Lucent Technologies Inc, Case No 07-cv-2301 (DDC Dec 21, 2007)ECF no 1	7.2
United States v. JGC Corp No 11-cv-260 (SD Tex Apr 6 2011) ECF No 1	7.2

UNITED KINGDOM

Bank of credit commerce International SA v. Ali (No 2) 2000 1 CR 1354	1.4.4

EUROPEAN COURT OF HUMAN RIGHTS CASES

Belgian Linguistic Case, (1979 -80) 1 EHRR 252	4.2, 5.2, 9.4
Engel and Others v. The Netherlands (No.1) (1979-80) 1 EHRR 647	4.2.2, 5.2.2, 9.4.2
National Union of Belgian Police v. Belgium (1979 -80) 1 EHRR 578	4.2.2, 4.2.2.2, 4.2.2.3, 5.2.2
Swedish Engine Driver's Union v. Sweden (1979-80) 1 EHRR, 617	4.2.2, 5.2.2, 9.4.2
The Republic of Ireland v. The United Kingdom (1979-80) 2 EHRR 25	4.2.2, 5.2.2, 9.4.2

TABLES OF LEGISLATION

REFERENCES ARE TO PARAGRAPH NUMBERS

NIGERIA

PRIMARY LEGISLATION

Administration of Criminal Justice Law 2011, Laws of Lagos State	8.4.1
Corrupt Practices and other Related Offences Act 2000	7.1.3
Criminal Code Act 2004 (as amended)	4.3.3
Economic and Financial Crimes Commission (Establishment) Act 2004	8.4.1
Money Laundering Prohibition Act 2011 (as amended)	2.1.1

SECONDARY LEGISLATION

CBN (Anti-Money Laundering and Combating the Financing of Terrorism in Banks and other Financial Institutions in Nigeria) Regulations 2013	2.1.1

TERTIARY LEGISLATION

Anti-Money Laundering/Combating the Financing of Terrorism (AML/CFT) Reporting Guidelines 2012	2.1.1

UNITED STATES

PRIMARY LEGISLATION

Federal Rules of Criminal Procedure 2010	8.4.2
Foreign Corrupt Practices Act of 1977 (FCPA) 15 U.S.C	3.2.2, 7.1.2, 7.2
Securities Exchange Act 1934	7.3
The Currency and Foreign Transactions Reporting Act	2.1.2, 2.3.1

of 1970 (which legislative framework is commonly referred to as the 'Bank Secrecy Act' or 'BSA') (as amended)	
Uniting and Strengthening America by Providing Appropriate Tools Required To Intercept and Obstruct Terrorism (USA PATRIOT ACT) ACT of 2001	2.1.2, 4.1.2

SECONDARY LEGISLATION

Codified Bank Secrecy Act Regulations 2010, 31 CFR Chapter X (Effective March 1, 2011)	2.1.2
Section 312 of the US Patriot Act Final Regulation and Notice of Proposed Rule Making 2005	4.1.2

TERTIARY LEGISLATION

Bank Secrecy Act/Anti-Money Laundering Examination Manual 2010	1.1, 1.2, 1.3, 2.1.2, 9.4.1
Bank Secrecy Act/Anti-Money Laundering Examination Manual for Money Service Businesses 2008,	2.1.2

UNITED KINGDOM

PRIMARY LEGISLATION

Bribery Act 2010	7.1.1
Financial Services and Markets Act 2000	11.4.1
Proceeds of Crime Act 2002 (as amended)	2.1.3

SECONDARY LEGISLATION

Money Laundering Regulations 2007,	2.1.3

TERTIARY LEGISLATION

Bribery Act 2010: Joint Prosecution Guidance of the Director of the Serious Fraud Office and the Director of Public	7.3

Prosecutions

Bribery Act 2010 Guidance about procedures which relevant commercial organisations can put in place to prevent associated persons with them from bribing March 2011	7.1.1
Financial Conduct Authority Handbook, Senior Management Arrangements, Systems and Controls (SYSC)	6.1.3, 6.3.1
Financial crime: a guide for firms part 1: A firm's guide to preventing financial crime by the Financial Services Authority 2012	7.2
Financial Crime: a guide for firms Part 2: A firm's guide to preventing financial crime by the Financial Conduct Authority April 2013	7.2
Joint Money Laundering Steering Group JMLSG, Prevention of money laundering/combating terrorist financing, 2013 Revised Version, Guidance for the UK financial sector Part I Amended November 2013	9.1.3, 9.2.3, 9.3.3

REPUBLIC OF KOREA

PRIMARY LEGISLATION

Republic of Korea Criminal Act, No 293, Sep 18 1953 as last amended by Act No 10259 April 15 2010	7.3
The Act on Preventing Bribery of Foreign Public Officials in International Business Transactions (FBPA) 1998	7.3

AUSTRALIA

PRIMARY LEGISLATION

Australia's Criminal Code Act 1995	7.3

EUROPEAN UNION

SECONDARY LEGISLATION

Directive 2005/60/EC of the European Parliament and of the council of 26th October 2005 on the prevention of the use of the financial system for the purpose of money laundering and terrorist financing OJ 2005 L309/15	1.4.1.2, 1.4.3.2, 1.4.3.3, 1.4.4

TABLE OF INTERNATIONAL CONVENTIONS

REFERENCES ARE TO PARAGRAPH NUMBERS

African Charter on Human and Peoples Rights 1981	4.2, 5.2, 7.3
American Convention on Human Rights 1969	4.2, 5.2
European Convention on Human Rights 1950 as amended	4.2, 5.2
OECD Convention on Combating Bribery of Foreign Officials in International Business Transactions 1997	7.3
FATF Guidance on the Risk Based Approach to combating money laundering and terrorist financing, (High Level principles and procedures) 2007	1.4.3.4
Financial Action Task Force (FATF): International Standards on Combating Money Laundering and the financing of terrorism and proliferation, (The FATF Recommendations) 2012	2.0, 3.0
Financial Action Task Force on Money Laundering, the Forty Recommendations 1996	2.3.1
Forty Recommendations of the Financial Action Task Force on Money Laundering 1990	2.3.1
Universal Declaration of Human Rights 1948	3.5.1
United Nations Convention against Corruption 2004	7.3
United Nations Convention against Illicit Traffic in Narcotic Drugs and Psychotropic Substances, 1988	3.1
United Nations Convention against Transnational Organized Crime and the Protocol There to 2004,	3.1

LIST OF ABBREVIATIONS

AML: Anti Money Laundering

BCCI: Bank of Credit and Commerce International

BNIs: Bearer Negotiable Instruments

BSA: Bank Secrecy Act

CBN: Central Bank of Nigeria

CBP: Cross Border Protection

CDD: Customer Due Diligence

CFT: Combating the Financing of Terrorism

CTRs: Currency Transaction Reports

DNFBP: Designated non-financial businesses and professions (DNFBPs)

EFCC: Economic and Financial Crimes Commission

EDD: Enhanced Due Diligence

FATF: Financial Action Task Force

FCA: Financial Conduct Authority

FCPA: Foreign Corrupt Practices Act

FINCEN: Financial Crimes Enforcement Network

FIU: Financial Intelligence Unit

FSB: Financial Stability Board

HIDTA: High Intensity Drug Trafficking Areas

HIFCA: High Intensity Financial Crime Areas

IAIS: International Association of Insurance Supervisors

IMF: International Monetary Fund

IOSCO: International Organization of Securities Commissions

JMLSG: Joint Money Laundering Steering Group

MLPA: Money Laundering Prohibition Act

NCA: National Crime Agency

OFAC: Office of Foreign Assets Control

PEPs: Politically Exposed Persons

SAR: Suspicious Activity Report

SFO: Serious Fraud Office

STRs: Suspicious Transaction Reports

SYSC: Senior Management Arrangements, Systems and Controls

TTF: Topical Trust Funds

UDHR: Universal Declaration of Human Rights

UNODC: United Nations Office on Drugs and Crime

CHAPTER 1

INTRODUCTION TO MONEY LAUNDERING AND TERRORIST FINANCING

Money laundering and terrorist financing are financial crimes with potentially devastating social and financial effects. From the profits of the narcotics trafficker to the assets looted from government coffers by dishonest foreign officials, criminal proceeds have the power to corrupt and ultimately destabilize communities or entire economies. Terrorist networks are able to facilitate their activities if they have financial means and access to the financial system. In both money laundering and terrorist financing, criminals can exploit loopholes and other weaknesses in the legitimate financial system to launder criminal proceeds, finance terrorism, or conduct other illegal activities, and ultimately, hide the actual purpose of their activity.[1]

1.1 WHAT IS MONEY LAUNDERING?

Money laundering is the criminal practice of processing ill-gotten gains, or 'dirty' money, through a series of transactions; in this way the funds are 'cleaned' so that they appear to be proceeds from legal activities.[2]

---

[1] Federal Financial Institutions Examination Council: *Bank Secrecy Act/Anti-Money Laundering Examination Manual* 2010, 11.
[2] Federal Financial Institutions Examination Council: *Bank Secrecy Act/Anti-Money Laundering Examination Manual* 2010, 12.

Money laundering requires an underlying, primary, profit-making crime (such as corruption, drug trafficking, market manipulation, fraud, tax evasion, along with the intent to conceal the proceeds of the crime or to further the criminal enterprise. These activities generate financial flows that involve the diversion of resources away from economically- and socially-productive uses—and these diversions can have negative impacts on the financial sector. They also have a corrosive, corrupting effect on society and the economic system as a whole.[3]

Money laundering takes many forms, including:

i. Trying to turn money raised through criminal activity into 'clean' money (that is, classic money laundering;

ii. Handling the benefit of acquisitive crimes such as theft, fraud and tax evasion;

iii. Handling stolen goods;

iv. Being directly involved with any criminal or terrorist property, or entering into arrangements to facilitate the laundering of criminal or terrorist property; and

v. Criminals investing the proceeds of their crimes in the whole range of financial products.[4]

1.2 STAGES OF MONEY LAUNDERING

Although money laundering is a diverse and often complex process, it basically involves three independent steps that can occur simultaneously;

---

[3] International Monetary Fund, 'Anti-Money Laundering/Combating the Financing of Terrorism' (https://www.imf.org) https://www.imf.org/external/np/leg/amlcft/eng/ Accessed 28th September 2014.

[4] The Joint Money Laundering Steering Group JMLSG, *Prevention of money laundering/ combating terrorist financing* 2013 Revised Version, Guidance for the UK financial sector Part I, Amended November 2013, 7.

1.2.1 PLACEMENT

The first and most vulnerable stage of laundering money is placement. The goal is to introduce the unlawful proceeds into the financial system without attracting the attention of financial institutions or law enforcement. Placement techniques include structuring currency deposits in amounts to evade reporting requirements or commingling currency deposits of legal and illegal enterprises.[5]

This can be done when a person deposits an amount below ten thousand US dollars in the bank. The intention would be to evade reporting requirements.

It is worth noting that Banks are mandated to file Currency Transaction Reports when a person deposits an amount equivalent to ten thousand US dollars or more than ten thousand US dollars.

1.2.2 LAYERING

The second stage of the money laundering process is layering, which involves moving funds around the financial system, often in a complex series of transactions to create confusion and complicate the paper trail.[6]

A person who was successful in the placement stage is likely to move to this stage which appears to be more complex.

Such a person is likely to transfer part of the amount deposited, into other accounts to avoid being detected.

---

[5] Federal Financial Institutions Examination Council: *Bank Secrecy Act/ Anti-Money Laundering Examination Manual* 2010, 12.
[6] Ibid.

1.2.3 INTEGRATION

The ultimate goal of the money laundering process is integration. Once the funds are in the financial system and insulated through the layering stage, the integration stage is used to create the appearance of legality through additional transactions. These transactions further shield the criminal from a recorded connection to the funds by providing a plausible explanation for the source of the funds.[7]

This could happen when a person who deposited illegal funds in the bank withdraws the money and uses the money to purchase a house or any other movable or immovable property.

1.3 TERRORIST FINANCING

The motivation behind terrorist financing is ideological as opposed to profit-seeking, which is generally the motivation for most crimes associated with money laundering. Terrorism is intended to intimidate a population or to compel a government or an international organization to do or abstain from doing any specific act through the threat of violence. An effective financial infrastructure is critical to terrorist operations.[8]

Terrorist groups develop sources of funding that are relatively mobile to ensure that funds can be used to obtain material and other logistical items needed to commit terrorist acts. Thus, money laundering is often a vital component of terrorist financing.

Terrorists generally finance their activities through both unlawful and legitimate sources. Unlawful activities, such as extortion, kidnapping, and narcotics trafficking, have been found to be a

[7] Ibid.
[8] Ibid.

major source of funding. Other observed activities include smuggling, fraud, theft, robbery, identity theft, use of conflict diamonds, and improper use of charitable or relief funds. In the last case, donors may have no knowledge that their donations have been diverted to support terrorist causes.

Other legitimate sources have also been found to provide terrorist organizations with funding; these legitimate funding sources are a key difference between terrorist financiers and traditional criminal organizations. In addition to charitable donations, legitimate sources include foreign government sponsors, business ownership, and personal employment.

Although the motivation differs between traditional money launderers and terrorist financiers, the actual methods used to fund terrorist operations can be the same as or similar to those methods used by other criminals that launder funds. For example, terrorist financiers use currency smuggling, structured deposits or withdrawals from bank accounts; purchases of various types of monetary instruments; credit, debit, or prepaid cards; and funds transfers. There is also evidence that some forms of informal banking (e.g., "hawala" have played a role in moving terrorist funds. Transactions through hawalas are difficult to detect given the lack of documentation, their size, and the nature of the transactions involved. Funding for terrorist attacks does not always require large sums of money, and the associated transactions may not be complex.[9]

---

[9] Federal Financial Institutions Examination Council: *Bank Secrecy Act/Anti-Money Laundering Examination Manual* 2010, 13.

1.4 ANTI-MONEY LAUNDERING RISK ASSESSMENT

Financial institutions and designated non-financial businesses and professions (DNFBPs are required to take appropriate steps to assess their money laundering and terrorist financing risks.

A well-developed risk assessment will assist in identifying the bank's Anti-Money Laundering (AML risk profile. Understanding the risk profile enables the bank to apply appropriate risk management processes to the AML compliance programme to mitigate risk. This risk assessment process enables management to better identify and mitigate gaps in the bank's controls. The risk assessment should provide a comprehensive analysis of the AML risks in a concise and organized presentation and should be shared and communicated with all business lines across the bank, board of directors, management, and appropriate staff; as such, it is a sound practice that the risk assessment be reduced to writing.[10]

The development of the AML risk assessment generally involves two steps: first, identify the specific risk categories (i.e., products, services, customers, entities, transactions, and geographic locations unique to the bank; and second, conduct a more detailed analysis of the data identified to better assess the risk within these categories.[11]

1.4.1 IDENTIFICATION OF SPECIFIC RISK CATEGORIES

The first step of the risk assessment process is to identify the specific products, services, customers, entities, and geographic

[10] Federal Financial Institutions Examination Council: *Bank Secrecy Act/Anti-Money Laundering Examination Manual* 2010, 22.
[11] Ibid.

locations unique to the bank. Although attempts to launder money, finance terrorism, or conduct other illegal activities through a bank can emanate from many different sources, certain products, services, customers, entities, and geographic locations may be more vulnerable or have been historically abused by money launderers and criminals. Depending on the specific characteristics of the particular product, service, or customer, the risks are not always the same. Various factors, such as the number and volume of transactions, geographic locations, and nature of the customer relationships, should be considered when the bank prepares its risk assessment. The differences in the way a bank interacts with the customer (face-to-face contact versus electronic banking also should be considered. Because of these factors, risk will vary from one bank to another.[12]

1.4.1.1 Products And Services

Certain products and services offered by banks may pose a higher risk of money laundering or terrorist financing depending on the nature of the specific product or service offered. Such products and services may facilitate a higher degree of anonymity, or involve the handling of high volumes of currency or currency equivalents. Some of these products and services includes amongst others; Private Banking, Electronic Funds Payment Services, Trade Finance and Foreign Exchange.[13]

1.4.1.2 Customers And Entities

The amount of corruption and abuse of public funds by some government leaders and public officials over recent years have given great cause for concern both internationally as well as in

---

[12] Federal Financial Institutions Examination Council: *Bank Secrecy Act/Anti-Money Laundering Examination Manual* 2010, 23.
[13] Federal Financial Institutions Examination Council: *Bank Secrecy Act/Anti-Money Laundering Examination Manual* 2010, 24.

countries involved. Those people are collectively known as politically exposed persons (PEPs. [14] PEPs are individuals who are or have been entrusted with prominent public functions and an immediate family member or a known close associate of such a person.[15]

There are special challenges in entering into financial transactions and business relationships with PEPs. Typical customer due diligence (CDD measures may prove insufficient for PEPs as financial transactions and business relationships with these individuals present a higher money laundering risk and hence require greater scrutiny than "normal" financial transactions and business accounts.[16]

Other customers/entities that may pose a higher money laundering risk includes amongst others: money service businesses, casinos, card clubs, brokers/dealers in securities, non-resident aliens (NRA, off shore corporations and non-governmental organizations.[17]

1.4.1.3 Geographic Locations

Identifying geographic locations that pose a higher risk is essential to a bank's AML compliance programme. Financial

---

[14] D Hopton, *Money Laundering A Concise Guide for All Business* (2nd Edition Gower 2009) 108

[15] The Financial Action Task Force (FATF): International Standards on Combating Money Laundering and the financing of terrorism and proliferation, (The FATF Recommendations) 2012, Recommendation 12.

See also Directive 2005/60/EC of the European Parliament and of the council of 26th October 2005 on the prevention of the use of the financial system for the purpose of money laundering and terrorist financing Article 3 (8). See also Money Laundering Regulations 2007/2157 Regulation 14 (5). See also the Joint Money Laundering Steering Group *Guidance for the UK Financial Sector* Part 1, Paragraph 5.5.19.

[16] KKR Choo, *'Politically exposed persons (PEPs): risk and mitigation'* 2008, 11 (4) JMLC, 371 – 387'

[17] Federal Financial Institutions Examination Council: *Bank Secrecy Act/Anti-Money Laundering Examination Manual 2010,* 25.

institutions/DNFBPs should understand and evaluate the specific risk associated with doing business in, opening accounts for customers from, or facilitating transactions involving certain geographic locations.[18]

Higher-risk geographic locations can be either international or domestic. International higher-risk geographic locations generally include: Countries subject to the Office of Foreign Assets Control (OFAC sanctions, including state sponsors of terrorism, Jurisdictions or countries monitored for deficiencies in their regimes to combat money laundering and terrorist financing by international entities such as the Financial Action Task Force (FATF. [19]

Domestic higher-risk geographic locations include: High Intensity Drug Trafficking Areas (HIDTA and High Intensity Financial Crime Areas (HIFCA [20]

1.4.2 ANALYSIS OF SPECIFIC RISK CATEGORIES

The second step of the risk assessment process entails a more detailed analysis of the data obtained during the identification stage in order to more accurately assess AML risk.

This step involves evaluating data pertaining to the bank's activities (e.g., number of: domestic and international funds transfers; private banking customers; foreign correspondent accounts; and domestic and international geographic locations of the bank's business area and customer transactions in relation to CDD information.

---

[18] Federal Financial Institutions Examination Council: *Bank Secrecy Act/Anti-Money Laundering Examination Manual* 2010, 25.
[19] Federal Financial Institutions Examination Council: *Bank Secrecy Act/Anti-Money Laundering Examination Manual* 2010, 26.
[20] Federal Financial Institutions Examination Council: *Bank Secrecy Act/Anti-Money Laundering Examination Manual* 2010, 26, 27.

The detailed analysis is important because within any type of product or category of customer there will be account holders that pose varying levels of risk.

Specifically, the analysis of the data pertaining to the bank's activities should consider, as appropriate, the following factors:

i. Purpose of the account;

ii. Actual or anticipated activity in the account;

iii. Nature of the customer's business/occupation;

iv. Customer's location;

v. Types of product and services used by the customer.[21]

1.4.3 DEVELOPING THE BANK'S AML COMPLIANCE PROGRAMME BASED UPON ITS RISK ASSESSMENT

Management should structure the bank's AML compliance programme to adequately address its risk profile, as identified by the risk assessment.

The bank's monitoring systems to identify, research, and report suspicious activity should be risk-based, with particular emphasis on higher-risk products, services, customers, entities and geographic locations as identified by the bank's AML risk assessment.[22]

This section explains in more detail how the risk-based approach can be applied.

It explains this by using PEPs as an example.

---

[21] Federal Financial Institutions Examination Council: *Bank Secrecy Act/Anti-Money Laundering Examination Manual* 2010, 27.

[22] Federal Financial Institutions Examination Council: *Bank Secrecy Act/Anti-Money Laundering Examination Manual* 2010, 28.

1.4.3.1 Customer Due Diligence

Customer Due Diligence/know your customer is intended to enable a financial institution to form a reasonable belief that it knows the true identity of each customer and, with an appropriate degree of confidence, knows the type of transactions the customer is likely to undertake.[23]

Failure of firms taking adequate steps to identify PEPs may lead to corrupt PEPs opening accounts without being detected and in the process avoiding enhanced due diligence and on-going monitoring. For example, in the late 1980's a large multinational bank in London opened accounts for Ibrahim and Mohamed Sani Abacha, who represented themselves as ''Commodity and Oil dealers" The bank failed to make note of the Father's position at the time as a General in the Army. By the late 1990's it was discovered that the two brothers had amassed and deposited, either for themselves or on behalf of others, approximately six hundred and sixty million dollars with the London bank. It was later revealed that Sani Abacha brothers and other members of the Abacha circle had allegedly stolen an estimated four billion, three hundred million dollars over a number of years.[24]

Another example is the Abubakar Atiku's case. According to the US subcommittee on investigations (2010 report, Abubakar used a variety of schemes through wire transfers to launder suspected funds into the United States. In many cases, these accounts were disguised by using the variant of his wife's name (Ms Douglas. The bank's profile did not identify Ms Douglas as a PEP.[25]

---

23 FATF Guidance on the Risk Based Approach to combating money laundering and terrorist financing, (High Level principles and procedures) 2007, paragraph 3.10.

24 OJ Otusanya: *'The Role of offshore financial centres in elite money laundering practices: evidence from Nigeria',* 2012,15(3) JMLC, 336 – 361.

25 OJ Otusanya: *'The Role of offshore financial centres in elite money laundering practices: evidence from Nigeria.* 2012', 15(3) JMLC, 336 – 361.

In situations where the money laundering risk associated with the business relationship is increased, for example where the customer is a PEP, banks must carry out additional enhanced due diligence.[26]

1.4.3.2 Enhanced Due Diligence

The Enhanced Due Diligence (EDD should give firms a greater understanding of the customer and their associated risk than standard due diligence. It should provide more certainty that the customer and/or beneficial owner is who they say they are and that the purposes of the business relationship are legitimate; as well as increasing opportunities to identify and deal with concerns that they are not.[27]

It is for each firm to decide the steps it takes to determine whether a PEP is seeking to establish a business relationship for legitimate reasons. Firms should in any case take adequate meaningful measures to establish the source of funds and source of wealth. Firms may wish to refer to information sources such as asset and income declarations, which some jurisdictions expect certain senior public officials to file and which often include

---

[26] The Financial Action Task Force (FATF): International Standards On Combating Money Laundering and the financing of terrorism and proliferation,(The FATF Recommendations) 2012, Recommendation 12, See also Directive 2005/60/EC of the European Parliament and of the council of 26th October 2005 on the prevention of the use of the financial system for the purpose of money laundering and terrorist financing Article 13 (1), See also Money Laundering Regulations 2007/2157 Regulation 14 (1), see also Uniting and Strengthening America by Providing Appropriate Tools Required to Intercept and Obstruct Terrorism Act 2001, s 312 (1).

[27] Financial crime: a guide for firms part 1: A firm's guide to preventing financial crime by the Financial Services Authority 2012 Box 3.7. See also Uniting and Strengthening America by Providing Appropriate Tools Required to Intercept and Obstruct Terrorism Act 2001 S 312 (2) (B) I, ii which states that the enhanced due diligence policies and procedures enables firms in the United States to ascertain for any such foreign bank, the shares of which are not publicly traded, the identity of each owners of the foreign bank and the nature and extent of the ownership interest of each such owner.

information about an official's source of wealth and current business interests. Firms should note that not all declarations are publicly available and that a PEP customer may have a legitimate reason for not providing a copy.[28] In countries where the declarations ought to be publicly available and are not still available for example countries like Nigeria who just signed an agreement committing to publication of asset declaration with the U.S. Government,[29] firms should insist that they see the declaration and if they are not given the declaration they should not open the account. It is worth noting that despite the agreement being signed, President Goodluck Jonathan has refused to publicly declare his assets.[30] This poses problems for firms.

Once the source of wealth and source of funds are established, banks will need to analyse the information for "red flag" for corrupt PEP activity.[31] In all cases if a bank suspects that the funds are proceeds of criminal activity, the bank is required to file a Suspicious Transaction Report with the Financial Intelligence Unit.[32] A risk based approach for the reporting of suspicious activity under these circumstances is not applicable.[33] A risk based approach is however appropriate for the purpose of identifying suspicious activity, for example by directing additional resources

---

[28] Joint Money Laundering Steering Group *Guidance for the UK Financial Sector* Part 1, Paragraph 5.5.28.

[29] O Aigbovo: *Nigerian anti-corruption statutes: an impact assessment* 2013 16 (1) JMLC 62 – 78.

[30] O Aigbovo: *Nigerian anti-corruption statutes: an impact assessment* 2013 16 (1) JMLC 62 – 78.

[31] T S Greenberg: *Stolen Asset Recovery, Politically Exposed Persons, A policy paper on strengthening preventive measures.*

[32] T S Greenberg: *Stolen Asset Recovery, Politically Exposed Persons, A policy paper on strengthening preventive measures.*

[33] FATF Guidance on the Risk Based Approach to combating money laundering and terrorist financing, (High Level principles and procedures) 2007, paragraph 3.16.

at those areas a financial institution has identified as higher risk and in this case to customers who are identified as PEPs.[34]

1.4.3.3 Senior Management Approval

The FATF standard requires banks to obtain senior management approval for establishing a business relationship with PEPs and continuing a business relationship with a customer who is subsequently found to be a PEP or becomes a PEP.[35] The group's Anti-Money Laundering and Countering Financing of Terrorism (AML/CTF officer should be involved in the PEP approval process since he is in the best position to say that a person should not be accepted regardless of the size of the account.[36]

1.4.3.4 Enhanced Ongoing Monitoring

Once a business relationship has been established with a PEP, banks must conduct enhanced on-going monitoring of the business relationship. [37]

The principle aim of monitoring in a risk based system is to respond to enterprise wide issues based on each financial

---

[34] FATF Guidance on the Risk Based Approach to combating money laundering and terrorist financing, (High Level principles and procedures) 2007, paragraph 3.17.

[35] The Financial Action Task Force (FATF): International Standards On Combating Money Laundering and the financing of terrorism and proliferation, (The FATF Recommendations) 2012, Recommendation 12, See also Directive 2005/60/EC of the European Parliament and of the council of 26th October 2005 on the prevention of the use of the financial system for the purpose of money laundering and terrorist financing Article 13 (4) (b), See also Money Laundering Regulations 2007/2157 Regulation 14 (4) (a).

[36] T S Greenberg: *Stolen Asset Recovery, Politically Exposed Persons, A policy paper on strengthening preventive measures.*

[37] The Financial Action Task Force (FATF): International Standards On Combating Money Laundering and the financing of terrorism and proliferation, (The FATF Recommendations) 2012, Recommendation 12, See also Directive 2005/60/EC of the European Parliament and of the council of 26th October 2005 on the prevention of the use of the financial system for the purpose of money laundering and terrorist financing Article 13 (4) (d), See also Money Laundering Regulations 2007/2157 Regulation 14 (4) (c).

institution's analysis of major risks and in this case the major risks are PEPs.[38]

1.4.4 IMPLICATIONS OF FAILURE OF A FIRM TO CONDUCT ENHANCED DUE DILIGENCE (EDD) AND ENHANCED ONGOING MONITORING (EOM)

Firms who do not conduct the required EDD and EOM with PEPs are likely to be fined by the financial supervisor in the jurisdiction concerned. For example, In March 2012, the UK Financial Conduct Authority (FCA fined Coutts and Company eight million seven hundred and fifty thousand pounds for failing to establish and maintain effective AML systems and controls in relation to their high-risk customers including PEPs. Coutts failed to adequately assess the level of money laundering risk posed by PEPs and also failed to gather sufficient information to establish PEPs such as source of funds and source of wealth.[39]

In May 2012, FCA also fined Habib Bank five hundred and twenty-five thousand pounds and its MLRO seventeen thousand, five hundred pounds for failing to conduct adequate enhanced due diligence on higher risk customers.[40]

Failure of a bank to conduct EDD and EOM may lead to funds being laundered and regulators shutting the bank down as a result of that. An example is the Bank of Credit and Commerce International (BCCI scandal where the bank's UK operation was closed on 19th July 1991 due to the fact that money was being

[38] FATF Guidance on the Risk Based Approach to combating money laundering and terrorist financing, (High Level principles and procedures) 2007, paragraph 3.13.
[39] Financial crime: a guide for firms part 1: A firm's guide to preventing financial crime by the Financial Services Authority 2012 Box 3.15.
[40] Financial crime: a guide for firms part 1: A firm's guide to preventing financial crime by the Financial Services Authority 2012 Box 3.16.

laundered through the bank.[41] The rise and fall of BCCI was the greatest scandal in the history of banking.[42] The bank became insolvent because of the fraud perpetrated by staffs of the bank who allowed money to be laundered. This also affected the reputation of the bank and public confidence.

1.5 INTERNATIONAL BODIES/ORGANISATIONS

This section of the chapter highlights the different international bodies charged with fighting money laundering.

1.5.1 FINANCIAL ACTION TASK FORCE

The Financial Action Task Force (FATF is an inter-governmental body established in 1989 by the Ministers of its Member jurisdictions. The objectives of the FATF are to set standards and promote effective implementation of legal, regulatory and operational measures for combating money laundering, terrorist financing and other related threats to the integrity of the international financial system. The FATF is therefore a "policy-making body" which works to generate the necessary political will to bring about national legislative and regulatory reforms in these areas.

The FATF has developed a series of Recommendations that are recognised as the international standard for combating of money laundering and the financing of terrorism and proliferation of weapons of mass destruction. They form the basis for a co-ordinated response to these threats to the integrity of the financial system and help ensure a level playing field. First issued in 1990, the FATF Recommendations were revised in 1996, 2001, 2003

---

[41] P Alldridge *Money Laundering Law, Forfeiture, Confiscation, Civil Recovery, Criminal Laundering and Taxation of the proceeds of crime.* (Hart Publishing 2003) 38.

[42] Bank of credit commerce International SA v. Ali (No 2) 1999 4 ALL ER 83.

and most recently in 2012 to ensure that they remain up to date and relevant, and they are intended to be of universal application.

The FATF monitors the progress of its members in implementing necessary measures, reviews money laundering and terrorist financing techniques and counter-measures, and promotes the adoption and implementation of appropriate measures globally. In collaboration with other international stakeholders, the FATF works to identify national-level vulnerabilities with the aim of protecting the international financial system from misuse.

The FATF's decision making body, the FATF Plenary, meets three times per year.[43]

1.5.2 BASEL COMMITTEE

The Basel Committee (the committee) is the primary global standard-setter for the prudential regulation of banks and provides a forum for cooperation on banking supervisory matters. Its mandate is to strengthen the regulation, supervision and practices of banks worldwide with the purpose of enhancing financial stability. Mr Stefan Ingves Governor of Sveriges Riksbank, is the chairman of the Basel Committee. He was appointed as Basel Committee chairman in July 2011 and has been reappointed until June 2017.[44]

The committee has a long-standing commitment to promote the implementation of sound AML/CFT policies and procedures that are critical in protecting the safety and soundness of banks and the integrity of the international financial system.

---

[43] Financial Action Task Force, *'About us'* (http://www.fatf-gafi.org) http://www.fatf-gafi.org/pages/aboutus/ Accessed 10th September 2014.

[44] Basel Committee on Banking Supervision, *'About the Basel Committee'* (http://www.bis.org 20th June 2014) http://www.bis.org/bcbs/about.htm Accessed 10th September 2014.

Following an initial statement in 1988, it has published several documents in support of this commitment. In September 2012, the committee reaffirmed its stance by publishing the revised version of the core principles for effective banking supervision, in which a dedicated principle (BCP 29) deals with the abuse of financial services.[45]

1.5.3 THE WOLFSBERG GROUP OF INTERNATIONAL FINANCIAL INSTITUTIONS

The Wolfsberg Group is an association of eleven global banks, which aims to develop financial services industry standards, and related products, for Know Your Customer, Anti-Money Laundering and Counter Terrorist Financing policies.

The Group came together in 2000, at the **Château Wolfsberg** in north-eastern Switzerland, in the company of representatives from Transparency International, including Stanley Morris, and Professor Mark Pieth of the University of Basel, to work on drafting anti-money laundering guidelines for Private Banking. The Wolfsberg Anti-Money Laundering Principles for Private Banking were subsequently published in October 2000, revised in May 2002 and again most recently in June 2012.

The Group then published a Statement on the Financing of Terrorism in January 2002, and also released the Wolfsberg Anti-Money Laundering Principles for Correspondent Banking in November 2002 and the Wolfsberg Statement on Monitoring Screening and Searching in September 2003. In 2004, the Wolfsberg Group focused on the development of a due diligence model for financial institutions, in co-operation with Banker's

---

[45] Basel Committee on Banking Supervision: *Sound management of risks related to money laundering and financing of terrorism 2014,* Paragraph 2.

Almanac, thereby fulfilling one of the recommendations made in the Correspondent Banking Principles.

During 2005 and early 2006, the Wolfsberg Group of banks actively worked on four separate papers, all of which aim to provide guidance with regard to a number of areas of banking activity where standards had yet to be fully articulated by lawmakers or regulators. It was hoped that these papers would provide general assistance to industry participants and regulatory bodies when shaping their own policies and guidance, as well as making a valuable contribution to the fight against money laundering. The papers were all published in June 2006, and consisted of two sets of guidance: Guidance on a Risk Based Approach for Managing Money Laundering Risks and AML Guidance for Mutual Funds and Other Pooled Investment Vehicles. Also published were FAQs on AML issues in the Context of Investment and Commercial Banking and FAQs on Correspondent Banking, which complement the other sets of FAQs available on the site: on Beneficial Ownership, Politically Exposed Persons and Intermediaries.

In early 2007, the Wolfsberg Group issued its Statement against Corruption, in close association with Transparency International and the Basel Institute on Governance. It describes the role of the Wolfsberg Group and financial institutions more generally in support of international efforts to combat corruption. The Statement against Corruption identifies some of the measures financial institutions may consider in order to prevent corruption in their own operations and protect themselves against the misuse of their operations in relation to corruption. Shortly thereafter, the Wolfsberg Group and The Clearing House Association LLC issued a statement endorsing measures to enhance the transparency of international wire transfers to promote the effectiveness of global anti-money laundering and anti-terrorist financing programmes.

In 2008, the Group decided to refresh its 2003 FAQs on PEPs, followed by a reissued Statement on Monitoring, Screening & Searching in 2009. 2009 also saw the publication of the first Trade Finance Principles and Guidance on Credit/Charge Card Issuing and Merchant Acquiring Activities. The Trade Finance Principles were expanded upon in 2011 and the Wolfsberg Group also replaced its 2007 Wolfsberg Statement against Corruption with a revised, expanded and renamed version of the paper: Wolfsberg Anti-Corruption Guidance. This Guidance takes into account a number of recent developments and gives tailored advice to international financial institutions in support of their efforts to develop appropriate Anti-Corruption programmes, to combat and mitigate bribery risks associated with clients or transactions and also to prevent internal bribery.

Most recently, focus has expanded to the emergence of new payment methods and the Group published Guidance on Prepaid & Stored Value Cards, which considers the money laundering risks and mitigants of physical Prepaid and Stored Value Card Issuing and Merchant Acquiring Activities, and supplements the Wolfsberg Group Guidance on Credit/Charge Card Issuing and Merchant Acquiring Activities of 2009.[46]

1.5.4 INTERNATIONAL MONETARY FUND

The International Monetary Fund (IMF) is an organization of 188 countries, working to foster global monetary cooperation, secure financial stability, facilitate international trade, promote

[46] Wolfsberg Group, *'Global Banks: Global Standards'* (http://www.wolfsberg-principles.com/) http://www.wolfsberg-principles.com/ Accessed 28th September 2014.

high employment and sustainable economic growth, and reduce poverty around the world.[47]

During the past 14 years, the IMF's efforts in the area of AML helped shape domestic and international AML/CFT policies. They included over 70 AML/CFT assessments, multiple involvements in Article IV consultations and inputs into the design and implementation of financial integrity-related measures in Fund-supported programs, as well as a large number of capacity development activities, and research projects. The IMF's broad experience in exercising surveillance over members' economic systems, conducting financial sector assessments, and providing capacity development to its member countries has been particularly helpful in providing financial integrity advice in the context of surveillance, evaluating countries' compliance with the international AML/CFT standard and in developing programs to help them address identified shortcomings.

In line with a growing recognition of the importance of financial integrity issues for the IMF, the AML/CFT program has evolved over the years. In 2004, the Executive Board agreed to make AML/CFT assessments and capacity development activities a regular part of IMF work. On June 1, 2011, the Executive Board discussed a report reviewing the evolution of the IMF's AML/CFT program over the past five years and provided guidance as to how to move forward in this area.

Following up on the Executive Board discussion, on December 14, 2012, a Guidance Note on the inclusion of AML/CFT in surveillance and financial stability assessments (FSAs) was issued. It provides a framework to deal with cases where money laundering, terrorism financing, and related crimes are so serious

---

[47] International Monetary Fund, *'About the IMF'* (http://www.imf.org) http://www.imf.org/external/about/ourwork.htm Accessed 10th September 2014.

as to threaten domestic stability, balance of payments stability, the effective operation of the international monetary system—in the case of Article IV surveillance, or the stability of the domestic financial system—in the case of FSAs.

On March 12, 2014, the Board reviewed the Fund's AML/CFT strategy. It notably (i) endorsed the revised FATF AML/CFT standard and assessment methodology, (ii) encouraged staff to continue its efforts to integrate financial integrity issues into its surveillance and in the context of Fund-supported programs, when financial integrity issues are critical to financing assurances or to achieve program objectives, and (iii) decided that AML/CFT issues should continue to be addressed in all FSAPs but on a more flexible basis.

With respect to capacity development, in April 2009, the IMF launched a donor-supported trust fund—the first in a series of Topical Trust Funds (TTF)—to finance capacity development in AML/CFT. This first phase ended in April 2014. In light of the success of the program and of continuing high demand for capacity development in this area, a new five-year phase of the TTF started in May 2014 for a new five-year period. Donors (France, Japan, Luxembourg, the Netherlands, Norway, Qatar, Saudi Arabia, Switzerland and the United Kingdom) have together pledged more than twenty million dollars over the next five years to support this new Phase. As of August 2014, nine projects have already started under the second phase. The TTF complements existing accounts that finance the IMF's AML/CFT capacity development activities in member countries.[48]

[48] International Monetary Fund, *'The IMF and the Fight Against Money Laundering and the Financing of Terrorism'* (https://www.imf.org 5th September 2014) https://www.imf.org/external/np/exr/facts/aml.htm Accessed 28th September 2014.

1.5.5 THE WORLD BANK

The World Bank is a vital source of financial and technical assistance to developing countries around the world. It is not a bank in the ordinary sense but a unique partnership to reduce poverty and support development. Established in 1944, the World Bank Group is headquartered in Washington, D.C.[49]

The World Bank and International Monetary Fund developed a unique Reference Guide to Anti-Money Laundering (AML and Combating the Financing of Terrorism (CFT in an effort to provide practical steps for countries implementing an AML/CFT regime in accordance with international standards. The Guide, authored by Paul Allan Schott, describes the global problem of money laundering and terrorist financing on the development agenda of individual countries and across regions. It explains the basic elements required to build an effective AML/CFT legal and institutional framework and summarizes the role of the World Bank and the International Monetary Fund in fighting money laundering and terrorist financing.

The primary objective of this joint Bank-Fund project is to ensure that the information contained in the Reference Guide is useful and easily accessible by developing countries that are working to establish and strengthen their policies against money laundering and the financing of terrorism. Additionally, this Guide is intended to contribute to global understanding of the devastating consequences of money laundering and terrorist financing on development growth, and political stability and to

[49] The World Bank, *'What we do'* (http://www.worldbank.org) http://www.worldbank.org/en/about/what-we-do Accessed 10th September 2014.

expand the international dialogue on crafting practical solutions to implement effective AML/CFT regimes.[50]

1.5.6 THE INTERNATIONAL ORGANIZATION OF SECURITIES COMMISSION

The International Organization of Securities Commissions (IOSCO, established in 1983, is the acknowledged international body that brings together the world's securities regulators and is recognized as the global standard setter for the securities sector. IOSCO develops, implements, and promotes adherence to internationally recognized standards for securities regulation, and is working intensively with the G20 and the Financial Stability Board (FSB on the global regulatory reform agenda.

IOSCO's membership regulates more than 95% of the world's securities markets. Its members include over 120 securities regulators and 80 other securities markets participants (i.e. stock exchanges, financial regional and international organizations etc.. IOSCO is the only international financial regulatory organization which includes all the major emerging markets jurisdictions within its membership.[51]

IOSCO has adopted the principle that regulators should require securities (including derivatives market intermediaries to have in place policies and procedures designed to minimize the risk of the use of an intermediary's business as a vehicle for money

[50] The World Bank, *'Comprehensive Reference Guide to AML/CFT'* (http://web.worldbank.org) http://web.worldbank.org/WBSITE/EXTERNAL/TOPICS/EXTFINANCIALSECTOR/EXTAML/0,,contentMDK:20746893~menuPK:2495265~pagePK:210058~piPK:210062~theSitePK:396512,00.html Accessed 10th September 2014.

[51] The International Organization of Securities Commissions, *'General Information'* (http://www.iosco.org) http://www.iosco.org/about/ Accessed 10th of September 2014.

laundering.[52] IOSCO subsequently endorsed principles to address the application of the client due diligence process in the securities industry (CIBO. [53]

1.5.7 INTERNATIONAL ASSOCIATION OF INSURANCE SUPERVISORS

The International Association of Insurance Supervisors (IAIS is a voluntary membership organization of insurance supervisors and regulators from more than 200 jurisdictions in nearly than 140 countries. In addition to its Members, more than 130 Observers representing international institutions, professional associations and insurance and reinsurance companies, as well as consultants and other professionals participate in IAIS activities.[54]

The IAIS has given AML and CFT high priority. In October 2003 the IAIS approved and issued the *Insurance core principles and methodology*, which revised the core principles for the supervision of insurers. Compliance with the Insurance Core Principles is required for a supervisory system to be effective. In accordance with Insurance Core Principle 28, the Recommendations of the FATF applicable to the insurance sector and to insurance supervision must be satisfied to reach this objective.[55]

---

52 The International Organization of Securities Commissions: Objectives and Principles of Securities Regulation 2003, Principle 8.5.

53 The International Organization of Securities Commissions: Principles on Client Identification and Beneficial Ownership for the Securities Industry 2004. See also The International Organization of Securities Commissions: Final Report, Anti Money Laundering Guidance for Collective Investment Schemes 2005, 3.

54 International Association of Insurance Supervisors, *'About the IAIS'* (http://www.iaisweb.org) http://www.iaisweb.org/About-the-IAIS-28 Accessed 10th September 2014.

55 International Association of Insurance Supervisors: Guidance Paper on Anti-Money Laundering and Combating the Financing of Terrorism October 2004, Paragraph 3.

1.5.8 TRANSPARENCY INTERNATIONAL

In 1993, a few individuals decided to take a stance against corruption and created Transparency International. Now present in more than 100 countries, the movement works relentlessly to stir the world's collective conscience and bring about change. Much remains to be done to stop corruption, but much has also been achieved, including:

i. the creation of international anti-corruption conventions
ii. the prosecution of corrupt leaders and seizures of their illicitly gained riches
iii. national elections won and lost on tackling corruption
iv. companies held accountable for their behaviour both at home and abroad.[56]

[56] 'Transparency International, Óverview' (http://www.transparency.org) http://www.transparency.org/whoweare/organisation Accessed 10th September 2014.

CHAPTER 2

REPORTING REQUIREMENTS

The Financial Action Task Force (FATF), the independent intergovernmental body that develops and promotes policies to protect the global financial system against money laundering, terrorist financing and financing the proliferation of weapons of mass destruction, advised countries to enact laws that mandate financial institutions and designated nonfinancial businesses and professions (DNFBPs) to file certain reports. These reports are to be filed when a financial institution or DNFBP suspects or has reasonable grounds to suspect that funds are the proceeds of a criminal activity or are related to terrorist financing.[57]

Although countries have followed the advice of the FATF, the reporting requirements in different countries are not the same. For example, Nigeria and the United States require financial institutions to file suspicious transaction reports (STRs) and currency transaction reports (CTRs),[58] while countries like the United Kingdom require financial institutions to file only a suspicious activity report (SAR).[59]

---

[57] The Financial Action Task Force (FATF): International Standards on Combating Money Laundering and the financing of terrorism and proliferation (The FATF Recommendations) (2012), Recommendation 20, 23.

[58] Money Laundering Prohibition Act 2011 (as amended), sections 6, 2 and 10. See also the Codified Bank Secrecy Act Regulations 2010, s 1020.320 (b) (1), s 1022.320 (b) (1) and s 1010.311.

[59] The Joint Money Laundering Steering Group JMLSG, *Prevention of Money Laundering/Combating Terrorist Financing* (2013) revised version, Guidance for the United Kingdom Financial Sector Part I, Amended November 2013, Paragraph 6.33. Please note that STR and SAR are the same even if the names are different. For more information, see E.P Ellinger, *Modern Banking Law,* 5th edition (Oxford University Press, 2011), 97.

This chapter, therefore, compares the reporting requirements in Nigeria with those of the United States and the United Kingdom. The aim of such comparison is to determine if Nigeria needs to adopt the approach in these countries or if there is no need for reform.

This chapter briefly highlights the relevant money laundering laws/regulations in Nigeria, the United States and the United Kingdom. It will then compare the reporting requirements in Nigeria with those of the United States and the United Kingdom under five subheadings: 'What to File', 'Where to File', 'When to File', 'Confidentiality of SARs' and 'Penalties'. The chapter will later analyse issues that arise from the earlier comparison, with the aim of determining if there is need for reform.

2.1 RELEVANT MONEY LAUNDERING LAWS/REGULATIONS

2.1.1 NIGERIA

The laws enacted to combat money laundering in Nigeria include: the **Money Laundering Prohibition Act 2011 (as amended), Central Bank of Nigeria (CBN) (Anti-Money Laundering and Combating the Financing of Terrorism in Banks and other Financial Institutions in Nigeria) Regulations 2013** and the **Anti-Money Laundering/Combating the Financing of Terrorism (AML/CFT) Reporting Guidelines 2012**.

2.1.2 UNITED STATES

The laws enacted to combat money laundering in the United States include: the **Currency and Foreign Transactions Reporting Act of 1970 (which legislative framework is commonly referred to as the 'Bank Secrecy Act' or 'BSA') as**

amended, Codified Bank Secrecy Act (BSA) Regulations 2010, the **Bank Secrecy Act/Anti-Money Laundering Examination Manual 2010** and the **Bank Secrecy Act/ Anti-Money Laundering Examination Manual for Money Service Businesses 2008.**

2.1.3 UNITED KINGDOM

The laws enacted to combat money laundering in the United Kingdom include: **Proceeds of Crime Act 2002 (as amended), Money Laundering Regulations 2007,** the **Financial Conduct Authority Handbook, Senior Management Arrangements, Systems and Controls (SYSC)** and the **Joint Money Laundering Steering Group JMLSG, Prevention of money laundering/combating terrorist financing, 2013 Revised Version, Guidance for the UK financial sector Part I Amended November 2013.**

2.2 REPORTING REQUIREMENTS

2.2.1 NIGERIA

2.2.1.1 What To File

A financial institution or designated non-financial institution is required to report any suspicious transaction.[60] A transaction is deemed to be suspicious if it involves a frequency which is unjustifiable or unreasonable[61] or is surrounded by conditions of unusual or unjustified complexity.[62] It is also deemed suspicious if it appears to have no economic justification or lawful objective[63] or in the opinion of the financial institution or

[60] Money Laundering Prohibition Act 2011 (as amended), s. 6 (2)
[61] Money Laundering Prohibition Act 2011 (as amended), s. 6 (1) (a)
[62] Money Laundering Prohibition Act 2011 (as amended), s. 6 (1) (b)
[63] Money Laundering Prohibition Act 2011 (as amended), s. 6 (1) (c)

designated non-financial institution involves terrorist financing or is inconsistent with the known transaction pattern of the account or business relationship.[64] The report required to be filed is called a Suspicious Transaction Report (STR).[65]

In addition to reporting any suspicious transaction, a financial institution or designated non-financial institution is also required to report a transfer to or from a foreign country of funds or securities by a person or body corporate including a money service business of a sum exceeding ten thousand US dollars or its equivalent.[66] The law also requires a financial institution or designated non-financial institution to report in writing any single transaction, lodgement or transfer of funds in excess of five million naira or its equivalent in the case of an individual or ten million naira or its equivalent in the case of a body corporate.[67] The report required to be filed is called a Currency Transaction Report (CTR).[68]

2.2.1.2 Where To File

A financial institution or a designated non-financial institution is required to file a STR with the Economic and Financial Crimes Commission (EFCC)[69]

A financial institution or a designated non-financial institution is also required to file a CTR with the Central Bank of Nigeria, Securities and Exchange Commission or the EFCC in writing.[70]

---

64 Money Laundering Prohibition Act 2011 (as amended), s. 6 (1) (d), See also the CBN (Anti-Money Laundering and Combating the Financing of Terrorism in Banks and Other Financial Institutions in Nigeria) Regulations, 2013, Regulation 31 (1) for the definition of a Suspicious Transaction.

65 Nigerian Financial Intelligence Unit: Anti-Money Laundering/Combating the Financing of Terrorism (AML/CFT) Reporting Guidelines 2012, Paragraph 2.

66 Money Laundering Prohibition Act 2011 (as amended), s. 2 (1)

67 Money Laundering Prohibition Act 2011 (as amended), s. 10 (1)

68 Nigerian Financial Intelligence Unit: Anti-Money Laundering/Combating the Financing of Terrorism (AML/CFT) Reporting Guidelines 2012, Paragraph 2.

69 Money Laundering Prohibition Act 2011 (as amended), s. 6 (2) (c)

2.2.1.3 When To File

A financial institution that suspects or has reason to suspect that funds are the proceeds of a criminal activity or are related to terrorist financing, is required to report its suspicions **immediately and without delay.**[71] The report is expected to be filed not later than within 24 hours.[72]

All suspicious transactions, including attempted transactions are to be reported regardless of the amount involved.[73]

The CTR on the other hand is to be filed within 7 days from the date of the transaction.[74]

2.2.1.4 Confidentiality Of STRs /Tipping Off (General Rule)

Financial institutions, their directors, officers and employees (permanent and temporary) are prohibited from disclosing the fact that a report is required to be filed with the competent authorities.[75]

2.2.1.5 Confidentiality Of STRs/Tipping Off (Exception)

There are no exceptions to the general rule.[76]

---

[70] Money Laundering Prohibition Act 2011 (as amended), s. 2 (1), s. (10) (1)
[71] Money Laundering Prohibition Act 2011 (as amended), s. 6 (2)
[72] CBN (Anti-Money Laundering and Combating the Financing of Terrorism in Banks and Other Financial Institutions in Nigeria) Regulations, 2013, Regulation 31 (3)
[73] CBN (Anti-Money Laundering and Combating the Financing of Terrorism in Banks and Other Financial Institutions in Nigeria) Regulations, 2013, Regulation 32 (7)
[74] Money Laundering Prohibition Act 2011 (as amended), s. 2 (1), s. 10 (1)
[75] Money Laundering Prohibition Act 2011 (as amended), s. 16 (1) (a)
[76] Money Laundering Prohibition Act 2011 (as amended), s. 16 (1) which provides for no exception to the General Rule

2.2.1.6 Penalties

A person who discloses the fact that a report is required to be filed is liable on conviction to imprisonment for a term of not less than two years or a fine of not less than ten million naira.[77]

A person who fails to file a STR or CTR would be liable to imprisonment for a term of not less than 3 years or a fine of ten million naira or to both, in the case of an individual and twenty-five million naira in the case of a body corporate.[78]

2.2.2 UNITED STATES

2.2.2.1 What To File

2.2.2.1.1 Banks

Every bank is required to file a report of any suspicious transaction relevant to a possible violation of law or regulation.[79] A transaction requires reporting if it is conducted or attempted by, at, or through the bank, it involves or aggregates at least five thousand dollars in funds or other assets, and the bank knows, suspects or has reason to suspect that:

i. The transaction involves funds derived from illegal activities or is intended or conducted in order to hide or disguise funds or assets derived from illegal activities (including, without limitation, the ownership, nature, source, location, or control of such funds or assets) as part of a plan to violate or evade any federal law or regulation or to avoid any transaction reporting requirement under federal law or regulation,

---

[77] Money Laundering Prohibition Act 2011 (as amended), s. 16 (2) (a)
[78] Money Laundering Prohibition Act 2011 (as amended), s. 16 (2) (b)
[79] Codified Bank Secrecy Act Regulations 2010, s. 1020.320 (a) (1)

ii. The transaction is designed to evade any requirements of this chapter or of any other regulations promulgated under the Bank Secrecy Act, or

iii. The transaction has no business or apparent lawful purpose or is not the sort in which the particular customer would normally be expected to engage, and the bank knows of no reasonable explanation for the transaction after examining the available facts, including the background and possible purpose of the transaction.[80]

A suspicious transaction shall be reported by completing a Suspicious Activity Report (SAR).[81]

In addition to filing of a SAR, Banks are required to file a report of each deposit, withdrawal, exchange of currency or other payment or transfer, by, through or to such financial institution which involves a transaction in currency of more than ten thousand US dollars. This report is referred to as a Currency Transaction Report.[82]

2.2.2.1.2 Money Service Businesses

Every money service business is required to file a report of any suspicious transaction relevant to a possible violation of law or regulation.[83] A transaction requires reporting if it is conducted or attempted by, at or through a money service business, involves or aggregates funds or other assets of at least two thousand dollars and the money service business knows, suspects or has reason to suspect that the transaction (or a pattern of transactions of which the transaction is a part):

---

[80] Codified Bank Secrecy Act Regulations 2010, s. 1020.320 (a) (2)
[81] Codified Bank Secrecy Act Regulations 2010, s. 1020.320 (b) (1)
[82] Codified Bank Secrecy Act Regulations 2010, s. 1010.311
[83] Codified Bank Secrecy Act Regulations 2010, s. 1022.320 (a) (1)

i. Involves funds derived from illegal activity or is intended or conducted in order to hide or disguise funds or assets derived from illegal activity (including without limitation, the ownership, nature, source, location, or control of such funds or assets) as part of a plan to violate or evade any federal law or regulation or to avoid any transaction reporting requirement under Federal law or regulation.

ii. Is designed, whether through structuring or other means, to evade any requirements of this chapter or of any other regulations promulgated under the Bank Secrecy Act, as amended.

iii. Serves no business or apparent lawful purpose, and the reporting money service business knows of no reasonable explanation for the transaction after examining the available facts, including the background and possible purpose of the transaction.

iv. Involves use of the money service business to facilitate criminal activity.[84]

A suspicious transaction shall be reported by completing a Suspicious Activity Report – MSB ('SAR-MSB')[85]

In addition to filing a SAR, a money service business is also required to file a report of each deposit, withdrawal, exchange of currency or other payment or transfer, by, through or to such financial institution which involves a transaction in currency of more than ten thousand dollars.[86]

---

84 Codified Bank Secrecy Act Regulations 2010, s. 1022.320 (a) (2)
85 Codified Bank Secrecy Act Regulations 2010, s. 1022.320 (b) (1)
86 Codified Bank Secrecy Act Regulations 2010, s. 1010.311

2.2.2.2 Where To File

2.2.2.2.1 Banks

The SAR is to be filed with the Financial Crimes Enforcement Network (FinCEN) in a central location, to be determined by FinCEN, as indicated in the instructions to the SAR.[87]

The CTR is to be filed with the Commissioner of Internal Revenue, unless otherwise specified.[88]

2.2.2.2.2 Money Service Businesses

The SAR-MSB is to be filed in a central location to be determined by FinCEN, as indicated in the instructions to the SAR-MSB.[89]

The CTR is to be filed with the Commissioner of Internal Revenue, unless otherwise specified.[90]

2.2.2.3 When To File

2.2.2.3.1 Banks

A bank is required to file a SAR no later than 30 calendar days after the date of initial detection by the bank of facts that may constitute a basis for filing a SAR. If no suspect was identified on the date of the detection of the incident requiring the filing, a bank may delay filing a SAR for an additional 30 calendar days to identify a suspect. In no case is reporting to be delayed more than 60 calendar days after the date of initial detection of a reportable transaction. In situations involving violations that require immediate attention, such as, for example, on-going money

[87] Codified Bank Secrecy Act Regulations 2010, s. 1020.320 (b) (2)
[88] Codified Bank Secrecy Act Regulations 2010, s. 1010.306 (a) (3)
[89] Codified Bank Secrecy Act Regulations 2010, s. 1022.320 (b) (2)
[90] Codified Bank Secrecy Act Regulations 2010, s. 1010.306 (a) (3)

laundering schemes, the bank shall notify by telephone, an appropriate law enforcement authority in addition to filing timely a SAR.[91]

A CTR is also required to be filed by the bank within 15 days following the day on which the reportable transaction occurred.[92]

2.2.2.3.2 Money Service Businesses

A money service business is required to file each SAR-MSB no later than 30 calendar days after the date of the initial detection by the money service business of facts that may constitute a basis for filing a SAR-MSB.[93]

A CTR is also required to be filed by the money service business within 15 days following the day on which the reportable transaction occurred.[94]

2.2.2.4 Confidentiality Of SARs/Tipping Off (General Rule)

2.2.2.4.1 Banks And Money Service Businesses

No bank/money service business and no director, officer, employee, or agent of any bank/money service business is to disclose a SAR or any information that would reveal the existence of a SAR. Any bank, and any director, officer, employee, or agent of any bank/money service business that is subpoenaed or otherwise requested to disclose a SAR or any information that would reveal the existence of a SAR, shall decline to produce the SAR or such information. The bank/money service business is

---

[91] Codified Bank Secrecy Act Regulations 2010, s. 1020.320 (b) (3)
[92] Codified Bank Secrecy Act Regulations 2010, s. 1010.306 (a) (1)
[93] Codified Bank Secrecy Act Regulations 2010, s. 1022.320 (b) (3)
[94] Codified Bank Secrecy Act Regulations 2010, s. 1010.306 (a) (1)

also to notify FinCEN of any such request and the response thereto.[95]

2.2.2.5 Confidentiality Of SARs/Tipping Off (Exceptions)

2.2.2.5.1 Banks And Money Service Businesses

The disclosure by a bank/money service business, or any director, officer, employee, or agent of a bank/money service business of:

i. A SAR, or any information that would reveal the existence of a SAR, to FinCEN or any Federal, State, or Local Law enforcement agency, or any Federal regulatory authority that examines the bank/money service business for compliance with the Bank Secrecy Act, or any State regulatory authority administering a State law that requires the bank/money service business to comply with the Bank Secrecy Act or otherwise authorizes the State authority to ensure that the bank/money service business complies with the Bank Secrecy Act;[96] or

ii. The underlying facts, transactions and documents upon which a SAR is based, including but not limited to, disclosures to another financial institution, or any director, officer, employee, or agent of a financial institution, for the preparation of a Joint SAR;[97] or

iii. The sharing by a bank/money service business, or any director, officer, employee, or agent of the bank/money service business, of a SAR, or any

[95] Codified Bank Secrecy Act Regulations 2010, s. 1020.320 (e) (1), s 1022.320 (d) (1)
[96] Codified Bank Secrecy Act Regulations 2010, s. 1020.320 (e) (1) (A) (1), s 1022.320 (d) (1) (A) (1)
[97] Codified Bank Secrecy Act Regulations 2010, s. 1020.320 (e) (1) (A) (2), s 1022.320 (d) (1) (A) (2)

information that would reveal the existence of a SAR, within the bank's/money service business's corporate organizational structure for purposes consistent with Title II of the Bank Secrecy Act as determined by regulation or in guidance is not prohibited.[98]

2.2.2.6 Penalties

2.2.2.6.1 Civil Penalty

i. For any wilful violation, committed on or before October 12, 1984, of any reporting requirement for financial institutions, the Secretary may assess upon any domestic financial institution, and upon any partner, director, officer, or employee thereof who wilfully participates in the violation, a civil penalty not to exceed one thousand dollars.[99]

ii. For any wilful violation committed after October 12, 1984 and before October 28, 1986, of any reporting requirement for financial institutions, the Secretary may assess upon any domestic financial institution, and upon any partner, director, officer, or employee thereof who wilfully participates in the violation, a civil penalty not to exceed ten thousand dollars.[100]

iii. For any wilful violation committed after October 27, 1986, of any reporting requirement for financial institutions under this part (except §103.24, §103.25 or §103.32), the Secretary may assess upon any domestic financial institution, and upon any partner, director,

---

[98] Codified Bank Secrecy Act Regulations 2010, s. 1020.320 (e) (1) (B), s 1022.320 (d) (1) (B)

[99] Codified Bank Secrecy Act Regulations 2010, s. 1010.820 (a)

[100] Codified Bank Secrecy Act Regulations 2010, s. 1010.820 (b)

officer, or employee thereof who wilfully participates in the violation, a civil penalty not to exceed the greater of the amount (not to exceed $100,000) involved in the transaction or twenty five thousand dollars.[101]

2.2.2.6.2 Criminal Penalty

Any person who violates any provision, may, upon conviction thereof, be fined not more than two hundred and fifty thousand dollars or be imprisoned not more than 5 years, or both.[102]

2.2.3 UNITED KINGDOM

2.2.3.1 What To File

A firm's nominated officer must report any transaction or activity that, after his evaluation, he knows or suspects, or has reasonable grounds to know or suspect, may be linked to money laundering or terrorist financing, or to attempted money laundering or terrorist financing.[103] Such report is called a Suspicious Activity Report.[104]

2.2.3.2 Where To File

To avoid committing a failure to report offence, nominated officers must make their disclosures to the National Crime

---

[101] Codified Bank Secrecy Act Regulations 2010, s. 1010.820 (f)
[102] Codified Bank Secrecy Act Regulations 2010, s. 1010.840 (b)
[103] Proceeds of Crime Act 2002 (as amended), s. 331, Money Laundering Regulations 2007, Regulation 20 (2) (d) and the Joint Money Laundering Steering Group JMLSG, *Prevention of money laundering/ combating terrorist financing,* 2013 Revised Version, Guidance for the UK financial sector Part I Amended November 2013, Paragraph 6.33.
[104] Joint Money Laundering Steering Group JMLSG, *Prevention of money laundering/ combating terrorist financing,* 2013 Revised Version, Guidance for the UK financial sector Part I Amended November 2013, Chapter 6, See also P Lilley, *Dirty Dealing: The Untold Truth About Global Money Laundering, International Crime and Terrorism* (3rd Edition, Kogan Page Limited, 2006) 209.

Agency (NCA). The national reception point for disclosure of suspicions, and for seeking consent to continue to proceed with the transaction or activity, is the UK Financial Intelligence Unit (FIU) within the NCA.[105]

2.2.3.3 When To File

Such reports must be made as soon as is reasonably practicable after the information comes to him.[106]

2.2.3.4 Confidentiality Of SARs/Tipping Off (General Rule)

A person is not to disclose a SAR if such disclosure is likely to prejudice any investigation that might be conducted following the disclosure and the information on which the disclosure is based came to the person in the course of a business in the regulated sector.[107]

2.2.3.5 Confidentiality Of SARs/Tipping Off (Exception)

i. An employee, officer or partner of an undertaking does not commit an offence if the disclosure is to an employee, officer or partner of the same undertaking.[108]

ii. A person does not commit an offence in respect of a disclosure by a credit institution or a financial institution if—

    a. The disclosure is to a credit institution or a financial institution,

---

[105] Joint Money Laundering Steering Group JMLSG, *Prevention of money laundering/ combating terrorist financing,* 2013 Revised Version, Guidance for the UK financial sector Part I Amended November 2013, Paragraph 6.40

[106] Joint Money Laundering Steering Group JMLSG, *Prevention of money laundering/ combating terrorist financing,* 2013 Revised Version, Guidance for the UK financial sector Part I Amended November 2013, Paragraph 6.33

[107] Proceeds of Crime Act 2002 (as amended), s. 333A (1)

[108] Proceeds of Crime Act 2002 (as amended), s. 333B (1)

b. The institution to whom the disclosure is made is situated in an EEA State or in a country or territory imposing equivalent money laundering requirements, and

c. Both the institution making the disclosure and the institution to which it is made belong to the same group.[109]

iii. A professional legal adviser or a relevant professional adviser does not commit an offence under section 333A if—

(a) The disclosure is to professional legal adviser or a relevant professional adviser,

(b) both the person making the disclosure and the person to whom it is made carry on business in an EEA State or in a country or territory imposing equivalent money laundering requirements, and

(c) Those persons perform their professional activities within different undertakings that share common ownership, management or control.[110]

2.2.3.6 Penalties

2.2.3.6.1 Tipping Off

A person guilty of the offence of tipping off is liable on summary conviction to imprisonment for a term not exceeding 3 months or to a fine not exceeding level 5 on the standard scale or to

---

109 Proceeds of Crime Act 2002 (as amended), s. 333B (2)

110 Proceeds of Crime Act 2002 (as amended), s. 333B (4), See also Proceeds of Crime Act 2002 (as amended), s 333C and D for more exceptions.

both[111] and on conviction on indictment, to imprisonment for a term not exceeding two years, or to a fine, or to both.[112]

2.2.3.6.2 Failure To File A SAR

A person guilty of not filing a SAR is liable on summary conviction for a term not exceeding 6 months or to a fine not exceeding the statutory maximum or to both,[113] and on conviction on indictment, to imprisonment for a term not exceeding five years or to a fine or to both.[114]

2.3 DISCUSSION

The previous section compared the reporting requirements in Nigeria with those of the United States and the United Kingdom. This section analyses the issues that arose from the comparison, with the aim of determining if there is need for reform.

2.3.1 WHAT TO FILE

As stated earlier, Nigerian and US money laundering laws require financial institutions to file currency transaction reports (CTRs) and suspicious transaction reports (STRs), while the United Kingdom's law requires that financial institutions file only suspicious activity reports (SARs). Is it necessary for Nigerian and US money laundering laws to mandate financial institutions to file CTRs since they are not required by the United Kingdom?

The question can be answered by looking briefly into the history behind the US Bank Secrecy Act. In 1970, Congress passed the Currency and Foreign Transactions Reporting Act, commonly known as the Bank Secrecy Act, which established requirements

111 Proceeds of Crime Act 2002 (as amended), s. 333A (4) (a)
112 Proceeds of Crime Act 2002 (as amended), s. 333A (4) (b)
113 Proceeds of Crime Act 2002 (as amended), s. 334 (2) (a)
114 Proceeds of Crime Act 2002 (as amended), s. 334 (2) (b)

for record keeping and reporting by private individuals, banks and other financial institutions. The Bank Secrecy Act was designed to help identify the source, volume and movement of currency and other monetary instruments transported or transmitted into or out of the United States or deposited in financial institutions. The statute requires individuals, banks and other financial institutions to file currency reports with the US Department of the Treasury, properly identify persons conducting transactions and maintain a paper trail by keeping appropriate records of financial transactions. These records enable law enforcement and regulatory agencies to pursue investigations of criminal tax and regulatory violations, if warranted, and provide evidence that is useful in prosecuting money laundering and other financial crimes.

In April 1996, a suspicious activity report (SAR) was developed to be used by all banking organizations in the United States. A banking organization is required to file a SAR whenever it detects a known or suspected criminal violation of federal law, a suspicious transaction related to money laundering activity or a violation of the Bank Secrecy Act.[115]

Legislators did not remove the CTR requirement, even though the SAR seeks to achieve the same objective, which is identifying the source, volume and movement of currency and preventing money laundering.

The international law the United States based its 1996 development on required financial institutions to file both a CTR and a STR.[116] This international law has been updated several

---

115 Federal Financial Institutions Examination Council: *Bank Secrecy Act/ Anti–Money Laundering Examination Manual* (2010), 7–8.

116 The Forty Recommendations of the Financial Action Task Force on Money Laundering (1990), Recommendations 16, 24; The Financial Action Task Force on Money Laundering, The Forty Recommendations (1996), Recommendations 15, 23.

times, with the most recent version requiring only an STR to be filed.[117]

Since the CTR requirement seeks to achieve a similar objective as the SAR requirement, it's no surprise that the UK money laundering law does not include the CTR requirement. This strengthens the argument that it may not be necessary for a financial institution to be required by law to file a CTR.

2.3.2 WHEN A TRANSACTION REQUIRES REPORTING

As stated earlier, the Nigerian and United Kingdom money laundering laws require all suspicious transactions, including attempted transactions, to be reported, regardless of the amount involved. This position is different from that of the US Bank Secrecy Act, which sets a particular threshold for reporting. This section of the chapter seeks to determine which of these requirements is preferable.

A threshold requirement appears to allow businesses to flourish because bank customers who engage in transactions below five thousand dollars will not have their transactions stalled by ongoing investigations. However, the threshold mechanism can be circumvented with techniques like smurfing.[118]

Therefore, the 'no threshold rule' is preferable.

2.3.3 CONFIDENTIALITY OF SARS

The Nigerian Money Laundering Prohibition Act 2011 (MLPA 2011) (as amended) provides no exceptions to the general rule of

---

[117] The Financial Action Task Force (FATF): International Standards on Combating Money Laundering and the financing of terrorism and proliferation, (The FATF Recommendations) 2012, Recommendation 20.

[118] Smurfing is the act of breaking down a transaction into smaller transactions to avoid regulatory requirements or an investigation by the authorities. http://financial-dictionary.thefreedictionary.com/Smurfing

tipping off, which is contrary to the positions of the United Kingdom and the United States. This section of the chapter seeks to determine if the tipping-off provision in MLPA 2011 needs to be amended to include detailed exceptions.

The tipping-off provision, as currently drafted, could cause serious problems for financial institutions and designated nonfinancial institutions. First, it is not clear if a disclosure by a financial institution to law enforcement agents is permitted. Second, it is not clear if a disclosure by a financial institution to another financial institution is permitted. Third, it is not clear if a disclosure by a professional legal adviser to another professional legal adviser is permitted. All these disclosures are stated in both the UK and US laws as clear exceptions to the general rule of tipping off.

In view of the above arguments, the tipping-off provision in MLPA 2011 needs to be amended to contain detailed exceptions like those of the United Kingdom and the United States.

2.4 CONCLUSION

This chapter compared the reporting requirements in Nigeria with those of the United States and the United Kingdom. It has also analysed issues that arose from the comparison to determine the need for reform. This section focuses on those areas that need reform.

Based on the arguments in Section 2.3 of this chapter, the following reforms to MLPA 2011 are recommended:

i. Sections two and ten of MLPA 2011 should be deleted, and section six should remain intact. In other words, firms should be required to file only STRs and should no longer be required to file CTRs.

ii. Section 16 (1) (a) of MLPA 2011 and Regulation 31 (6) of CBN (Anti–Money Laundering and Combating the Financing of Terrorism in Banks and other Financial Institutions in Nigeria) Regulations 2013 should be amended to include exceptions to the general rule of tipping off, as stated in the US Codified Bank Secrecy Act Regulations 2010.[119] Alternatively, the exceptions could be added to Section 333B, 333D (1) and (2) and 333D (3) of the United Kingdom's Proceeds of Crime Act 2002 (as amended).

[119] Codified Bank Secrecy Act Regulations (2010), s. 1020.320 (e) (1) (A) (1), s. 1022.320 (d) (1) (A) (1), s. 1020.320 (e) (1) (A) (2), s. 1022.320 (d) (1) (A) (2), s. 1020.320 (e) (1) (B), s. 1022.320 (d) (1) (B).

CHAPTER 3

MONEY LAUNDERING OFFENCE

The Financial Action Task Force (FATF) has advised countries to do the following: (i) criminalize money laundering; (ii) apply the crime of money laundering to all serious offences, with a view to including the widest range of predicate offences; (iii) extend predicate offences for money laundering to conduct that occurred in another country when it would have constituted a predicate offence had it occurred domestically and (iv) apply effective, proportionate and dissuasive criminal sanctions to natural persons convicted of money laundering.[120]

While countries followed the advice of the FATF by criminalizing money laundering and have implemented all the above recommendations, the approaches taken by these countries are different.

This chapter compares the approaches taken by Nigeria with those of the United States and the United Kingdom under four subheadings: 'The Crime of Money Laundering', 'Predicate Offences for Money Laundering (Domestic Crimes)', 'Predicate Offences for Money Laundering (Foreign Crimes)' and 'Penalties'. This chapter will also analyse issues that arise from the comparison to determine if there is need for reform.

---

[120] The Financial Action Task Force (FATF): International Standards on Combating Money Laundering and the Financing of Terrorism and Proliferation, (The FATF Recommendations) 2012, Interpretive Note to Recommendation 3

3.1 THE CRIME OF MONEY LAUNDERING

The FATF has advised countries to criminalise money laundering on the basis of the **United Nations Convention against Illicit Traffic in Narcotic Drugs and Psychotropic Substances 1988 (the Vienna Convention)** and the **United Nations Convention against Transnational Organized Crime, 2000 (the Palermo Convention).**[121]

The Vienna Convention requires each party to adopt such measures as may be necessary to establish as criminal offences under its domestic law, when committed intentionally:

i. The conversion or transfer of property, knowing that such property is derived from any offence or offences established in accordance with **subparagraph (a) of paragraph 1 (Article 3)**, or from an act of participation in such offence or offences, for the purpose of concealing or disguising the illicit origin of the property or of assisting any person who is involved in the commission of such an offence or offences to evade the legal consequences of his actions;[122]

ii. The concealment or disguise of the true nature, source, location, disposition, movement, rights with respect to, or ownership of property, knowing that such property is derived from an offence or offences established in accordance with **subparagraph (a) of paragraph 1 (Article 3)** or from an act of participation in such an offence or offences;[123]

---

[121] Ibid.

[122] United Nations Convention Against Illicit Traffic in Narcotic Drugs and Psychotropic Substances, 1988, Article 3 (1) (b) (i)

[123] United Nations Convention Against Illicit Traffic in Narcotic Drugs and Psychotropic Substances, 1988, Article 3 (1) (b) (ii)

iii. The acquisition, possession or use of property, knowing, at the time of receipt, that such property was derived from an offence or offences established in accordance with or from an act of participation in such offence or offences;[124]

iv. The possession of equipment or materials or substances listed in Table I and Table II, knowing that they are being or are to be used in or for the illicit cultivation, production or[125]

v. Publicly inciting or inducing others, by any means, to commit any of the offences established in accordance with this article or to use narcotic drugs or psychotropic substances illicitly;[126]

vi. Participation in, association or conspiracy to commit, attempts to commit and aiding, abetting, facilitating and counselling the commission of any of the offences established in accordance with this article.[127]

Subparagraph (a) of paragraph 1 (Article 3) of the Vienna Convention lists the following offences:

i. The production, manufacture, extraction; preparation, offering, offering for sale, distribution, sale, delivery on any terms whatsoever, brokerage, dispatch, dispatch in transit, transport, importation or exportation of any narcotic drug or any psychotropic substance contrary

---

124 United Nations Convention Against Illicit Traffic in Narcotic Drugs and Psychotropic Substances, 1988, Article 3 (1) (c) (i)

125 United Nations Convention Against Illicit Traffic in Narcotic Drugs and Psychotropic Substances, 1988, Article 3 (1) (c) (ii)

126 United Nations Convention Against Illicit Traffic in Narcotic Drugs and Psychotropic Substances, 1988, Article 3 (1) (c) (iii)

127 United Nations Convention Against Illicit Traffic in Narcotic Drugs and Psychotropic Substances, 1988, Article 3 (1) (c) (iv)

to the provisions of the 1961 Convention, the 1961 Convention as amended or the 1971 Convention;

ii. The cultivation of opium poppy, coca bush or cannabis plant for the purpose of the production of narcotic drugs contrary to the provisions of the 1961 Convention and the 1961 Convention as amended;

iii. The possession or purchase of any narcotic drug or psychotropic substance for the purpose of any of the activities enumerated in (i) above;

iv. The manufacture, transport or distribution of equipment, materials or of substances listed in Table I and Table II, knowing that they are to be used in or for the illicit cultivation, production or manufacture of narcotic drugs or psychotropic substances.

The Palermo Convention requires each State Party to adopt, in accordance with fundamental principles of its domestic law, such legislative and other measures as may be necessary to establish as criminal offences, when committed intentionally:

i. The conversion or transfer of property, knowing that such property is the proceeds of crime, for the purpose of concealing or disguising the illicit origin of the property or of helping any person who is involved in the commission of the predicate offence to evade the legal consequences of his or her action;[128]

ii. The concealment or disguise of the true nature, source, location, disposition, movement or ownership of or rights

[128] United Nations Convention Against Transnational Organized Crime and the Protocol There to 2004, Article 6 (1) (a) (i)

with respect to property, knowing that such property is the proceeds of crime.[129]

Subject to the basic concepts of its legal system:

iii. The acquisition, possession or use of property, knowing, at the time of receipt, that such property is the proceeds of crime;[130]

iv. Participation in, association with or conspiracy to commit, attempts to commit and aiding, abetting, facilitating and counselling the commission of any of the offences established in accordance with this article.[131]

Although countries have followed the advice of the FATF by criminalising money laundering on the basis of the Vienna Convention and the Palermo Convention, the approaches in these countries are different.

This section compares the approaches in Nigeria with those of the United States and the United Kingdom.

3.1.1 NIGERIA

The Nigerian Money Laundering Prohibition Act 2011 (as amended) makes it a money laundering offence for any person or body corporate in or outside Nigeria, to directly or indirectly:

i. Conceal or disguise the origin of;[132]

ii. Convert or transfer;[133]

iii. Remove from the jurisdiction; or[134]

---

[129] United Nations Convention Against Transnational Organized Crime and the Protocol There to 2004, Article 6 (1) (a) (ii)

[130] United Nations Convention Against Transnational Organized Crime and the Protocol There to 2004, Article 6 (1) (b) (i)

[131] United Nations Convention Against Transnational Organized Crime and the Protocol There to 2004, Article 6 (1) (b) (ii)

[132] Money Laundering Prohibition Act 2011 (as amended), s. 15 (2) (a)

[133] Money Laundering Prohibition Act 2011 (as amended), s. 15 (2) (b)

iv. Acquire, use, retain or take possession or control of;[135]

Any fund or property, knowingly or reasonably ought to have known that such fund or property is, or forms part of the proceeds of an unlawful act.[136]

A person also commits the offence of money laundering if he or she:

i. Conspires with, aids, abets or counsels any other person to commit the offence of money laundering;[137]

ii. Attempts to commit or is an accessory to an act or offence of money laundering; or[138]

iii. Incites, procures or induces any other person by any means whatsoever to commit the offence of money laundering.[139]

3.1.2 UNITED STATES

The U.S. Bank Secrecy Act (Statute) (1970) (as amended) is to the effect that:

(1) Whoever, knowing that the property involved in a financial transaction represents the proceeds of some form of unlawful activity, conducts or attempts to conduct such a financial transaction which in fact involves the proceeds of specified unlawful activity[140]—

(A)

---

134 Money Laundering Prohibition Act 2011 (as amended), s. 15 (2) (c)
135 Money Laundering Prohibition Act 2011 (as amended), s. 15 (2) (d)
136 Money Laundering Prohibition Act 2011 (as amended), s. 15 (2)
137 Money Laundering Prohibition Act 2011 (as amended), s. 18 (a)
138 Money Laundering Prohibition Act 2011 (as amended), s. 18(b)
139 Money Laundering Prohibition Act 2011 (as amended), s. 18 (c)
140 Bank Secrecy Act (Statute), s. 1956 (a) (1)

i. With the intent to promote the carrying on of specified unlawful activity; or[141]

ii. With intent to engage in conduct constituting a violation of section 7201 or 7206 of the Internal Revenue Code of 1986; or[142]

(B) Knowing that the transaction is designed in whole or in part—

i. To conceal or disguise the nature, the location, the source, the ownership, or the control of the proceeds of specified unlawful activity; or[143]

ii. To avoid a transaction reporting requirement under State or Federal law,[144]

Shall be guilty of the offence of money laundering

A financial transaction shall be considered to be one involving the proceeds of specified unlawful activity if it is part of a set of parallel or dependent transactions, any one of which involves the proceeds of specified unlawful activity, and all of which are part of a single plan or arrangement.[145]

(2) Also, whoever transports, transmits or transfers, or attempts to transport, transmit, or transfer a monetary instrument or funds from a place in the United States to or through a place outside the United States or to a place in the United States from or through a place outside the United States.[146]—

---

141 Bank Secrecy Act (Statute), s. 1956 (a) (1) (A) (i)
142 Bank Secrecy Act (Statute), s. 1956 (a) (1) (A) (ii)
143 Bank Secrecy Act (Statute), s. 1956 (a) (1) (B) (i)
144 Bank Secrecy Act (Statute), s. 1956 (a) (1) (B) (ii)
145 Bank Secrecy Act (Statute), s. 1956 (a) (1) (B)
146 Bank Secrecy Act (Statute), s. 1956 (a) (2)

(A) With the intent to promote the carrying on of specified unlawful activity; or[147]

(B) Knowing that the monetary instrument or funds involved in the transportation, transmission, or transfer represent the proceeds of some form of unlawful activity and knowing that such transportation, transmission, or transfer is designed in whole or in part[148]—

i. To conceal or disguise the nature, the location, the source, the ownership, or the control of the proceeds of specified unlawful activity; or[149]

ii. To avoid a transaction reporting requirement under State or Federal law,[150]

Shall be guilty of the offence of money laundering

(3) Whoever, with the intent—

i. To promote the carrying on of specified unlawful activity;[151]

ii. To conceal or disguise the nature, location, source, ownership, or control of property believed to be the proceeds of specified unlawful activity; or[152]

iii. To avoid a transaction reporting requirement under State or Federal law,[153]

Conducts or attempts to conduct a financial transaction involving property represented to be the proceeds of specified unlawful activity, or property used to conduct or facilitate specified

---

147 Bank Secrecy Act (Statute), s. 1956 (a) (2) (A)
148 Bank Secrecy Act (Statute), s. 1956 (a) (2) (B)
149 Bank Secrecy Act (Statute), s. 1956 (a) (2) (B) (i)
150 Bank Secrecy Act (Statute), s. 1956 (a) (2) (B) (ii)
151 Bank Secrecy Act (Statute), s. 1956 (a) (3) (A)
152 Bank Secrecy Act (Statute), s. 1956 (a) (3) (B)
153 Bank Secrecy Act (Statute), s. 1956 (a) (3) (C)

unlawful activity, shall be guilty of the offence of money laundering.

The term "represented" means any representation made by a law enforcement officer or by another person at the direction of, or with the approval of, a Federal official authorized to investigate or prosecute violations of this section.[154]

3.1.3 UNITED KINGDOM

The UK Proceeds of Crime Act 2002 (as amended) makes it a money laundering offence[155] for a person to:

i. Conceal criminal property;[156]

ii. Disguise criminal property;[157]

iii. Convert criminal property;[158]

iv. Transfer criminal property;[159]

v. Remove criminal property from England and Wales or from Scotland or from Northern Ireland;[160]

vi. Enter into or become concerned in an arrangement which he knows or suspects facilitates (by whatever means) the acquisition, retention, use or control of criminal property by or on behalf of another person;[161]

vii. Acquire criminal property;[162]

viii. Use criminal property;[163]

---

154 Bank Secrecy Act (Statute), s. 1956 (a) (3)

155 Proceeds of Crime Act 2002 (as amended), s. 340 (11) (a)

156 Proceeds of Crime Act 2002 (as amended), s. 327 (1) (a)

157 Proceeds of Crime Act 2002 (as amended), s. 327 (1) (b)

158 Proceeds of Crime Act 2002 (as amended), s. 327 (1) (c)

159 Proceeds of Crime Act 2002 (as amended), s. 327 (1) (d)

160 Proceeds of Crime Act 2002 (as amended), s. 327 (1) (e)

161 Proceeds of Crime Act 2002 (as amended), s. 328 (1)

162 Proceeds of Crime Act 2002 (as amended), s. 329 (1) (a)

ix. Have possession of criminal property;[164]

x. Attempt, conspire or incite another to commit the above offences;[165]

xi. Aid, abet, counsel or procure the commission of the above offences.[166]

The act of 'Entering into or becoming concerned in an arrangement which a person knows or suspects facilitates (by whatever means) the acquisition, retention, use or control of criminal property by or on behalf of another person' is not a money laundering offence in Nigeria and United States but it is a money laundering offence in the United Kingdom as stated above.

3.2 PREDICATE OFFENCES FOR MONEY LAUNDERING (DOMESTIC CRIMES)

The FATF has advised countries to apply the crime of money laundering to all serious offences, with a view to including the widest range of predicate offences.

According to the FATF, Predicate offences may be described by reference to all offences; or to a threshold linked either to a category of serious offences, or to the penalty of imprisonment applicable to the predicate offence (threshold approach); or to a list of predicate offences; or a combination of these approaches.[167]

This section compares the approaches in Nigeria with those of the United States and the United Kingdom.

[163] Proceeds of Crime Act 2002 (as amended), s. 329 (1) (b)
[164] Proceeds of Crime Act 2002 (as amended), s. 329 (1) (c)
[165] Proceeds of Crime Act 2002 (as amended), s. 340 (11) (b)
[166] Proceeds of Crime Act 2002 (as amended), s. 340 (11) (c)
[167] The Financial Action Task Force (FATF): International Standards on Combating Money Laundering and the Financing of Terrorism and Proliferation, (The FATF Recommendations) 2012, Interpretive Note to Recommendation 3

3.2.1 NIGERIA

The Nigerian Money Laundering Prohibition Act 2011 (as amended) applies the crime of money laundering to a list of predicate offences and also to any other criminal act specified in the Nigerian Money Laundering Law or any other law in Nigeria.[168]

The predicate offences listed in the Nigerian Money Laundering Law includes: participation in an organized criminal group, racketeering, terrorism, terrorist financing, trafficking in persons, smuggling of migrants, sexual exploitation, sexual exploitation of children, illicit trafficking in narcotic drugs and psychotropic substances, illicit arms trafficking, illicit trafficking in stolen goods, corruption, bribery, fraud, currency, counterfeiting, counterfeiting and piracy of products, environmental crimes, murder, grievous bodily injury, kidnapping, hostage taking, robbery or theft, smuggling (including in relation to customs and excise duties and taxes), extortion, forgery, piracy, insider trading and market manipulation.[169]

3.2.2 UNITED STATES

The U.S. Bank Secrecy Act (Statute) applies the crime of money laundering to a list of predicate offences.[170]

The predicate offences listed in the **U.S. Bank Secrecy Act (Statute)** include: an offence under section 32 (relating to the destruction of aircraft), section 37 (relating to violence at international airports), section 115 (relating to influencing, impeding, or retaliating against a Federal official by threatening or injuring a family member), section 152 (relating to

[168] Money Laundering Prohibition Act 2011 (as amended), s. 15 (6)
[169] Money Laundering Prohibition Act 2011 (as amended), s. 15 (6)
[170] Bank Secrecy Act (Statute), s. 1956 (c) (7) (A), (C), (D), (E) and (F)

concealment of assets; false oaths and claims; bribery), section 175c (relating to the variola virus), section 215 (relating to commissions or gifts for procuring loans), section 351 (relating to congressional or Cabinet officer assassination), any of sections 500 through 503 (relating to certain counterfeiting offenses), section 513 (relating to securities of States and private entities), section 541 (relating to goods falsely classified), section 542 (relating to entry of goods by means of false statements), section 545 (relating to smuggling goods into the United States.), section 549 (relating to removing goods from Customs custody), section 554 (relating to smuggling goods from the United States.), section 555 (relating to border tunnels), section 641 (relating to public money, property, or records), section 656 (relating to theft, embezzlement, or misapplication by bank officer or employee), section 657 (relating to lending, credit, and insurance institutions), section 658 (relating to property mortgaged or pledged to farm credit agencies), section 666 (relating to theft or bribery concerning programs receiving Federal funds), section 793, 794, or 798 (relating to espionage), section 831 (relating to prohibited transactions involving nuclear materials), section 844 (f) or (i) (relating to destruction by explosives or fire of Government property or property affecting interstate or foreign commerce), section 875 (relating to interstate communications), section 922 (l) (relating to the unlawful importation of firearms), section 924 (n) (relating to firearms trafficking), section 956 (relating to conspiracy to kill, kidnap, maim, or injure certain property in a foreign country), section 1005 (relating to fraudulent bank entries), 1006 [2] (relating to fraudulent Federal credit institution entries), 1007 [2] (relating to Federal Deposit Insurance transactions), 1014 [2] (relating to fraudulent loan or credit applications), section 1030 (relating to computer fraud and abuse), 1032 [2] (relating to concealment of assets from conservator, receiver, or liquidating agent of financial institution), section 1111 (relating to murder), section 1114 (relating to murder of United States law enforcement officials), section 1116 (relating to murder of foreign officials, official guests, or internationally protected persons), section 1201 (relating to kidnaping), section 1203 (relating to hostage taking), section 1361 (relating to wilful injury of Government property), section 1363 (relating to destruction of property within the special maritime and territorial jurisdiction), section 1708 (theft from the mail), section 1751 (relating to Presidential assassination), section 2113 or 2114 (relating to bank and postal robbery and theft), section 2252A (relating to child pornography) where the child pornography contains a visual depiction of an actual minor engaging in sexually explicit conduct, section 2260 (production of certain child pornography for importation into the United States), section 2280 (relating to violence against maritime navigation), section 2281 (relating to violence against maritime fixed platforms), section 2319 (relating to copyright infringement), section 2320 (relating to trafficking in counterfeit goods and services), section 2332 (relating to terrorist acts abroad against U.S. nationals), section 2332a (relating to use of weapons of mass destruction), section 2332b (relating to international terrorist acts transcending national boundaries), section 2332g (relating to missile systems designed to destroy aircraft), section 2332h (relating to radiological dispersal devices), section 2339A or 2339B (relating to providing material support to terrorists), section 2339C (relating to financing of terrorism), or section 2339D (relating to receiving military-type training from a foreign terrorist organization) of this title, section 46502 of title 49, U.S. Code, a felony violation of the Chemical Diversion and Trafficking Act of 1988 (relating to precursor and essential chemicals), section 590 of the Tariff Act of 1930 (19 U.S.C.

1590) (relating to aviation smuggling), section 422 of the Controlled Substances Act (relating to transportation of drug paraphernalia), section 38 (c) (relating to criminal violations) of the Arms Export Control Act, section 11 (relating to violations) of the Export Administration Act of 1979, section 206 (relating to penalties) of the International Emergency Economic Powers Act, section 16 (relating to offenses and punishment) of the Trading with the Enemy Act, any felony violation of section 15 of the Food and Nutrition Act of 2008 (relating to supplemental nutrition assistance program benefits fraud) involving a quantity of benefits having a value of not less than five thousand dollars, any violation of section 543(a)(1) of the Housing Act of 1949 (relating to equity skimming), any felony violation of the Foreign Agents Registration Act of 1938, any felony violation of the Foreign Corrupt Practices Act, or section 92 of the Atomic Energy Act of 1954 (42 U.S.C. 2122) (relating to prohibitions governing atomic weapons), environmental crimes,[171] a felony violation of the Federal Water Pollution Control Act (33 U.S.C. 1251 et seq.), the Ocean Dumping Act (33 U.S.C. 1401 et seq.), the Act to Prevent Pollution from Ships (33 U.S.C. 1901 et seq.), the Safe Drinking Water Act (42 U.S.C. 300f et seq.), or the Resources Conservation and Recovery Act (42 U.S.C. 6901 et seq.); or[172] any act or activity constituting an offence involving a Federal health care offense.[173]

Predicate offences also include any act or activity constituting an offence listed in section 1961 (1) of title 18 except an act which is indictable under subchapter II of chapter 53 of title 31;[174] and also any act or acts constituting a continuing criminal enterprise,

[171] Bank Secrecy Act (Statute), s. 1956 (c) (7) (D)
[172] Bank Secrecy Act (Statute), s. 1956 (c)(7) (E)
[173] Bank Secrecy Act (Statute), s. 1956 (c)(7) (F)
[174] Bank Secrecy Act (Statute), s. 1956 (c)(7) (A)

as that term is defined in section 408 of the Controlled Substances Act (21 U.S.C. 848);[175]

3.2.3 UNITED KINGDOM

The UK Proceeds of Crime Act 2002 (as amended) applies the crime of money laundering to all predicate offences.[176]

3.3 PREDICATE OFFENCES FOR MONEY LAUNDERING (FOREIGN CRIMES)

The FATF has advised countries to extend predicate offences for money laundering to conduct that occurred in another country, which constitutes an offence in that country, and which would have constituted a predicate offence had it occurred domestically (double criminality test).

According to the FATF, countries could also provide that the only prerequisite is that the conduct would have constituted a predicate offence, had it occurred domestically (single criminality test).[177]

This section compares the approaches in Nigeria with those of the United States and the United Kingdom.

3.3.1 NIGERIA

The Nigerian Money Laundering Prohibition Act 2011 (as amended) remains silent with regards to the application of the above tests.

---

175 Bank Secrecy Act (Statute), s. 1956 (c)(7) (C)

176 Proceeds of Crime Act 2002 (as amended), s. 340 (2) (a), See also The Joint Money Laundering Steering Group JMLSG, *Prevention of money laundering/ combating terrorist financing* 2013 Revised Version, Guidance for the UK financial sector Part I, Amended November 2013, Appendix II, Paragraph 1.

177 The Financial Action Task Force (FATF): International Standards on Combating Money Laundering and the Financing of Terrorism and Proliferation, (The FATF Recommendations) 2012, Interpretive Note to Recommendation 3

The reason for such silence could be as a result of the fact that the **Nigerian Criminal Code Act 2004** applies the single criminality test to offences partially committed in Nigeria.[178]

It could therefore be inferred from the above facts that the same test may be applied to 'predicate offences for money laundering' occurring outside Nigeria.

3.3.2 UNITED STATES

The United States extends predicate offences for money laundering to conduct that would have constituted a predicate offence, had it occurred domestically (single criminality test).

This test is therefore limited to a list of predicate offences and the value of funds involved in a transaction. The predicate offences include:

i. the manufacture, importation, sale, or distribution of a controlled substance (as such term is defined for the purposes of the Controlled Substances Act);[179]

ii. murder, kidnapping, robbery, extortion, destruction of property by means of explosive or fire, or a crime of violence (as defined in section 16);[180]

iii. fraud, or any scheme or attempt to defraud, by or against a foreign bank (as defined in paragraph 7 of section 1(b) of the International Banking Act of 1978));[181]

---

[178] Criminal Code Act 2004, s 12, See also F Nwadialo S.A.N, *The Criminal Procedure of the Southern States of Nigeria* (2nd Edition MIJ Professional Publishers Limited 1987) 14 – 15.

[179] Bank Secrecy Act (Statute), s. 1956 (c) (7) (B) (i)

[180] Bank Secrecy Act (Statute), s. 1956 (c) (7) (B) (ii)

[181] Bank Secrecy Act (Statute), s. 1956 (c) (7)(B) (iii)

iv. bribery of a public official, or the misappropriation, theft, or embezzlement of public funds by or for the benefit of a public official;[182]

v. smuggling or export control violations involving—

   a. an item controlled on the United States Munitions List established under section 38 of the Arms Export Control Act (22 U.S.C. 2778); or

   b. an item controlled under regulations under the Export Administration Regulations (15 C.F.R. Parts 730–774);[183]

vi. an offence with respect to which the US would be obligated by a multilateral treaty, either to extradite the alleged offender or to submit the case for prosecution, if the offender were found within the territory of the United States; or[184]

vii. trafficking in persons, selling or buying of children, sexual exploitation of children, or transporting, recruiting or harbouring a person, including a child, for commercial sex acts.[185]

The value involved in a transaction or series of related transactions includes funds or monetary instruments of a value exceeding ten thousand dollars.[186]

3.3.3 UNITED KINGDOM

The United Kingdom applies both the single criminality test and the double criminality test to conducts occurring abroad. The

---

182 Bank Secrecy Act (Statute), s. 1956 (c) (7) (B)(iv)
183 Bank Secrecy Act (Statute), s. 1956 (c) (7) (B) (v)
184 Bank Secrecy Act (Statute), s. 1956 (c) (7) (B) (vi)
185 Bank Secrecy Act (Statute), s. 1956 (c)(7) (B) (vii)
186 Bank Secrecy Act (Statute), s. 1956 (f)(2)

single criminality test is limited to predicate offences punishable for more than one year while the double criminality test is limited to predicate offences punishable for less than a year.[187]

3.4 PENALTIES

The FATF has advised countries to apply effective, proportionate and dissuasive criminal sanctions to natural persons convicted of money laundering.

The FATF has also advised countries to apply criminal liability and sanctions to legal persons and where that is not possible (due to fundamental principles of domestic law), civil or administrative liability and sanctions should apply.[188]

This section compares the approaches in Nigeria with those of the United States and the United Kingdom.

3.4.1 NIGERIA

A person who commits the offence of money laundering is liable on conviction to a term not less than 7 years but not more than 14 years imprisonment.[189]

A body corporate who commits the offence of money laundering is liable on conviction to a fine of not less than 100% of the funds and properties acquired as a result of the offence committed; and withdrawal of licence.[190]

---

187 Proceeds of Crime Act 2002, s. 340 (2) (b), See also Serious Organised Crime and Police Act 2005, s. 102 (1-7), The Proceeds of Crime Act 2002 (Money Laundering: Exceptions to Overseas Conduct Defence) Order 2006, Article 2

188 The Financial Action Task Force (FATF): International Standards on Combating Money Laundering and the Financing of Terrorism and Proliferation, (The FATF Recommendations) 2012, Interpretive Note to Recommendation 3

189 Money Laundering Prohibition Act 2011 (as amended), s. 15 (3)

190 Money Laundering Prohibition Act 2011 (as amended), s. 15 (4)

3.4.2 UNITED STATES

A person who commits the offence of money laundering shall be sentenced to a fine of not more than five hundred thousand dollars or twice the value of the property involved in the transaction, whichever is greater, or imprisonment for not more than twenty years, or both.[191]

3.4.3 UNITED KINGDOM

A person who commits the offence of money laundering is liable on summary conviction, to imprisonment for a term not exceeding six months or to a fine not exceeding the statutory maximum or to both,[192] or on conviction on indictment, to imprisonment for a term not exceeding 14 years or to a fine or to both.[193]

3.5 DISCUSSION

The previous section compared the approaches in Nigeria with those of the United States and the United Kingdom. This section will analyse issues that arose from the comparison to determine if there is need for reform.

3.5.1 PREDICATE OFFENCES FOR MONEY LAUNDERING (DOMESTIC CRIMES)

As stated earlier, the Nigerian Money Laundering Prohibition Act 2011 (as amended) applies the crime of money laundering to a list of predicate offences and also to any other criminal act specified in the money laundering law or any other law in Nigeria.

---

191 Bank Secrecy Act (Statute), s. 1956 (a) (1) (2) (3)
192 Proceeds of Crime Act 2002, s. 334 (1) (a)
193 Proceeds of Crime Act 2002, s. 334 (1) (b)

The United States, on the other hand, applies the crime of money laundering to a list of predicate offences, while the United Kingdom applies it to all predicate offences.

The US approach could be regarded as a good law to the extent that it applies the crime of money laundering to the most serious offences. However, the US approach violates Article 7 of the Universal Declaration of Human Rights (UDHR), which prohibits laws that discriminate against human beings.[194]

The discrimination is on the basis that people who commit less serious crimes are allowed to launder the proceeds generated from such crimes, while people who commit serious crimes or crimes not listed in the Bank Secrecy Act are not allowed to launder proceeds generated from such crimes.

The United Kingdom's approach, on the other hand, does not discriminate against persons, as it applies the crime of money laundering to all predicate offences.

Nigeria's approach is similar to that of the United Kingdom. The only difference is that it applies the crime of money laundering to a list of predicate offences. This is the case even when the same law also applies the crime of money laundering to all predicate offences.

In view of the above arguments, there is no need for Nigeria to apply the crime of money laundering to a list of predicate offences, since it is already applied to all offences.

---

[194] The Universal Declaration of Human Rights (1948), Article 7; F.F. Odibei, *Cases and Materials on Human Rights Law,* 1st edition (Pearl Publishers, 2011), 196–197.

3.5.2 PREDICATE OFFENCES FOR MONEY LAUNDERING (FOREIGN CRIMES)

The Nigerian Criminal Code Act 2004 applies the single criminality test to foreign crimes partially committed in Nigeria.

The United States, on the other hand, applies the single criminality test to serious crimes that are committed outside the United States. This test is, therefore, limited to the value of funds involved in a transaction.

The United Kingdom applies the single criminality test to serious crimes that are committed outside the United Kingdom. This test is not limited to any value of funds as it is in the United States.

The Nigerian approach appears to be in line with Article 2 (2) of the Vienna Convention, which mandates countries to carry out their obligations in a manner consistent with the principles of sovereign equality and territorial integrity of countries and that of nonintervention in the domestic affairs of other countries.

The US and UK approaches appear to be inconsistent with these principles. They both establish their jurisdictions over offences committed abroad, provided that the offence is a serious offence.

This approach is also inconsistent with Article 2 (3) of the Vienna Convention, which mandates that countries should not exercise jurisdiction and performance of functions in the territory of another country that are exclusively reserved for the authorities of that other country by its domestic law.

In view of the above arguments, the Nigerian approach is a good approach.

The United States and United Kingdom are advised to adopt the Nigerian approach by applying the single criminality test to foreign crimes partially committed within their jurisdictions.

3.6 CONCLUSION

This chapter compared the approaches in Nigeria with those of the United States and United Kingdom on the basis of the 'criminalization of money laundering' and other related subtopics. It has also analysed issues that arose from the comparison to determine if there is need for reform. This section focuses on those areas that need reform.

Based on the arguments canvassed in Section 3.5, the following reforms to the Nigerian Money Laundering Prohibition Act 2011 (as amended) are recommended:

I. The crime of money laundering should not be applied to a list of predicate offences since it is already applied to all offences.

II. The Nigerian Money Laundering Prohibition Act 2011 (as amended) should be amended to include the single criminality test, even if it is already included in the Nigerian Criminal Code Act.

CHAPTER 4

POLITICALLY EXPOSED PERSONS

Individuals who have, or have had, a high political profile and those who hold, or have held, public office can pose a higher money laundering risk, as their positions may make them vulnerable to corruption. These people are collectively known as politically exposed persons (PEPs).[195]

The risk associated with such individuals extends to members of their immediate families and to other known close associates. PEP status itself does not, of course, incriminate individuals or entities. It does, however, put the customer, or the beneficial owner, into a higher-risk category[196] that requires financial institutions to apply additional measures in order to reduce the risk.[197]

A PEP is defined as 'an individual who is or has, at any time in the preceding year, been entrusted with prominent public functions and an immediate family member, or a known close associate, of such a person'.[198]

---

195 The Joint Money Laundering Steering Group JMLSG, *Prevention of money laundering/combating terrorist financing 2013* Revised Version, Guidance for the UK financial sector Part I, Amended November 2013, Paragraph 5.5.18

196 Ibid.

197 The Financial Action Task Force (FATF): International Standards on Combating Money Laundering and the financing of terrorism and proliferation, (The FATF Recommendations) 2012, Recommendation 12

198 Money Laundering Prohibition Act 2011 (as amended), s. 25 (a) (b), See also Section 312 of the US Patriot Act Final Regulation and Notice of Proposed Rule Making 2005; Money Laundering Regulations 2007, Regulation 14 (5); JMLSG, *Prevention of Money Laundering*, Guidance for the United Kingdom Financial Sector Part I, Amended November 2013, Paragraph 5.5.19.

The Financial Action Task Force (FATF) requires that countries apply the PEP definition to only those holding such a position *outside* their jurisdictions.[199]

The United Nations Office on Drugs and Crime (UNODC), on the other hand, requires that countries apply the PEP definition to those holding such positions both inside and outside their jurisdictions.[200]

While some countries have adopted the approach of the FATF, others have adopted that of UNODC. For example, Nigeria applies the PEP definition to those holding such positions both inside and outside the country,[201] while the United States and United Kingdom apply the PEP definition to those holding such positions outside their respective countries.[202]

The best approach is one that strikes a balance between protecting the financial system against corrupt PEPs and upholding equality before the law.

4.1 APPLICATION OF THE PEPs DEFINITION

A PEP is defined as 'an **individual who is or has, at any time in the preceding year, been entrusted with prominent public functions** and **an immediate family member**, or a **known close associate**, of such a person'.[203]

[199] The Financial Action Task Force (FATF): International Standards on Combating Money Laundering and the financing of terrorism and proliferation, (The FATF Recommendations) 2012, Recommendation 12

[200] United Nations Convention against Corruption (2004), Article 52 (1)

[201] Money Laundering Prohibition Act 2011 (as amended), s. 25 (a) (b)

[202] USA Patriot Act of 2001: Uniting and Strengthening America By Providing Appropriate Tools Required To Intercept and Obstruct Terrorism, s. 312 (a) (3) (B); Money Laundering Regulations 2007, Regulation 14 (5) (a).

[203] The Financial Action Task Force (FATF): International Standards on Combating Money Laundering and the financing of terrorism and proliferation, (The FATF Recommendations) 2012, Recommendation 12

Individuals who are or have been entrusted with prominent public functions include: heads of state, heads of government, ministers and deputy, or assistant ministers, members of the Supreme Court, members of Courts of auditors or of the boards of central banks, ambassadors, charges d affairs and high-ranking officers in the armed forces, and members of the administrative, management or supervisory bodies of state owned enterprises. The categories above do not include middle-ranking or more junior officials.[204]

Immediate family members include: a spouse, a partner, children and their spouses or partners and parents.[205]

Persons known to be close associates include: any individual who is known to have joint beneficial ownership of a legal entity or legal arrangement, or any other close business relations with a person referred to as a PEP or any individual who has sole beneficial ownership of a legal entity or legal arrangement which is known to have been set up for the benefit of a person referred to as a PEP.[206]

Financial institutions are required to verify the identity of customers, to take reasonable steps to determine the identity of beneficial owners of funds deposited into high –value accounts and to conduct enhanced scrutiny of accounts sought or maintained by or on behalf of individuals who are, or have been, entrusted with prominent public functions and their family members and close associates. Such enhanced scrutiny shall be reasonably designed to detect suspicious transactions for the purpose of reporting to competent authorities and should not be

---

204 Money Laundering Regulations 2007, Schedule 2, Paragraph 4 (1) (a)
205 Money Laundering Regulations 2007, Schedule 2, Paragraph 4 (1) (c)
206 Money Laundering Regulations 2007, Schedule 2, Paragraph 4 (1) (d)

so construed as to discourage or prohibit financial institutions from doing business with any legitimate customer.[207]

This section will determine the approach that is being adopted by Nigeria, the United States and the United Kingdom with regards to the application of the definition of PEPs.

4.1.1 NIGERIA

Nigeria applies the PEP definition to those holding such a position inside and outside the country.[208]

4.1.2 UNITED STATES

The United States apply the PEP definition to those holding such positions outside the country.[209] The United States refers to PEPs as Senior Foreign Political Figures and limits the application of the definition to Senior Foreign Political Figures who maintain a private banking account with a U.S. financial institution.[210]

4.1.3 UNITED KINGDOM

The United Kingdom applies the PEP definition to those holding such a position outside the country.[211]

4.2 DISCUSSION

The previous section compared the approaches adopted in Nigeria, the United States and the United Kingdom with regard

---

[207] United Nations Convention Against Corruption 2004, Article 52 (1)

[208] Money Laundering Prohibition Act 2011 (as amended), s. 25 (a) (b)

[209] Uniting and Strengthening America By Providing Appropriate Tools Required To Intercept and Obstruct Terrorism (USA PATRIOT ACT) ACT of 2001, s. 312 (a) (3) (B)

[210] Uniting and Strengthening America By Providing Appropriate Tools Required To Intercept and Obstruct Terrorism (USA PATRIOT ACT) ACT of 2001, s. 312 (a) (3) (B), See also Section 312 of the US Patriot Act Final Regulation and Notice of Proposed Rule Making 2005

[211] Money Laundering Regulations 2007, Regulation 14 (5) (a)

to the application of the PEP definition. The best approach is one that strikes a balance between protecting the financial system against corrupt PEPs[212] and upholding equality before the law.[213]

4.2.1 PROTECTING THE FINANCIAL SYSTEM AGAINST CORRUPT PEPS

As stated earlier, Nigeria applies the PEP definition to those holding such positions inside and outside the country, while the United Kingdom and United States apply the definition only to those holding such positions outside the country. This section will determine which of the above approaches is more likely to protect the financial system against corrupt PEPs.

The Nigerian approach protects the financial system against individuals who are, or have been, entrusted with prominent public functions both inside and outside the country.

The US and UK approaches, on the other hand, protect the financial system against individuals who are or have been entrusted with prominent public functions outside their respective countries.

There appears to be no protection against individuals who are, or who have been, entrusted with prominent public functions within the United States and United Kingdom. However, such

---

[212] Transparency International, *'The Global Coalition against Corruption'* (http://www.transparency.org/cpi2013) http://www.transparency.org/cpi2013/results Accessed 26th June 2014.

[213] African Charter on Human and Peoples Rights (1981), Article 2; American Convention on Human Rights (1969), Article 1, 24; European Convention on Human Rights (1950) as amended, Article 14; J. Rehman, *International Human Rights Law,* 2nd edition (Pearson Education Limited, 2010), 214.

protection may not be needed since cases of corruption have been rare in these countries.[214]

4.2.2 UPHOLDING EQUALITY BEFORE THE LAW

This section will determine if the approaches adopted in Nigeria, the United States and United Kingdom directly violate the human rights of PEPs by looking into the conditions that must be cumulatively met in order to be considered direct discrimination. These conditions include differential treatment, prohibited grounds without objective and reasonable justification and no reasonable relationship of proportionality.[215]

4.2.2.1 Differential Treatment

One of the conditions that must exist in direct discrimination is that there must be a given difference in treatment, which may concern the exercise of any right set forth by law. [216]

The Nigerian approach does not create any difference in treatment concerning the exercise of any right set forth by law. It applies the PEP definition to those holding such positions both inside and outside Nigeria.

The US and UK approach, on the other hand, does create a difference in treatment concerning the exercise of certain rights set forth by law. Both countries require financial institutions to perform enhanced due diligence for individuals who are, or have

---

[214] Transparency International, *'The Global Coalition against Corruption'* (http://www.transparency.org/cpi2013) http://www.transparency.org/cpi2013/results Accessed 26th June 2014.

[215] Belgian Linguistic Case (1979 -80) 1 EHRR 252, Para 10; Swedish Engine Driver's Union v. Sweden (1979–80) 1 EHRR, 617, Para 45, 47, 48; National Union of Belgian Police v. Belgium (1979–80) 1 EHRR 578, Para 44, 46; Engel and Others v. The Netherlands (No.1) (1979–80) 1 EHRR 647, Para 72; The Republic of Ireland v. The United Kingdom (1979–80) 2 EHRR 25, Para 226.

[216] See Belgian Linguistic Case (1979–80) 1 EHRR 252, Para 10; National Union of Belgian Police v. Belgium (1979–80) 1 EHRR 578, Para 44, 46.

been, entrusted with prominent public functions in other countries. Such due diligence is not performed on individuals who are, or have been, entrusted with prominent public functions in the United Kingdom and United States.

Enhanced due-diligence measures could interfere with the private life of an individual when a financial institution, in trying to establish the source of income and source of wealth of a PEP, gets hold of information that the political figure never wanted anyone to see. The information could relate to that person's legitimate part-time business. This could definitely interfere with the PEP's private life.

The above scenario would not occur if the political figure held such a position in the United Kingdom or the United States.

Since the Nigerian approach does not create any difference in treatment with regard to PEPs, it does not directly discriminate against them. Therefore, there is no need to determine whether or not the Nigerian approach meets the other direct discrimination requirements.

4.2.2.2 Prohibited Grounds

The respective human rights conventions provide that discrimination could be on the grounds of sex, race, colour, national or social origin, property, birth or other status.[217] The US and UK approaches do discriminate on the grounds of a person's national origin.

[217] African Charter on Human and Peoples' Rights (1981) Article 2; American Convention on Human Rights, Article 1; European Convention on Human Rights (1950) as amended, Article 14.

4.2.2.3 Without Objective and Reasonable Justification

The third condition for an action to be considered direct discrimination is that the distinction or difference in treatment would have no objective and reasonable justification. The existence of such a justification must be assessed in relation to the aim and effects of the measure under consideration.[218] This means that we have to look at the aims and objectives in order to determine if the UK and US approaches have reasonable justification.

The aim of the application of the PEP definition to foreign individuals holding such positions is to reduce the risk of corrupt PEPs in countries where corruption is at a high level. The United Kingdom and the United States are not among these.[219]

Therefore, the US and UK approaches have objective and reasonable justifications.

4.2.2.4 No Reasonable Relationship of Proportionality

An individual's right to equality is likewise violated when it is clearly established that there is no reasonable relationship of proportionality between the means employed and the aim.[220] In other words, the state must strike a fair balance between the protection of the interests of the community and respect for the rights and freedoms safeguarded by the human rights convention.[221] Hence, if the measure in question creates no

[218] See Belgian Linguistic Case (1979–80) 1 EHRR 252, Para 10; National Union of Belgian Police v. Belgium (19790–80) 1 EHRR 578, Para 46.
[219] Transparency International, *'The Global Coalition against Corruption'* (http://www.transparency.org/cpi2013) http://www.transparency.org/cpi2013/results Accessed 26th June 2014.
[220] Belgian Linguistic Case (1979–80) 1 EHRR 252, Para 10; National Union of Belgian Police v. Belgium (1979–80) 1 EHRR 578, Para 46.
[221] See Belgian Linguistic Case (1979–80) 1 EHRR 252, Para 7.

impediment to the exercise of the individual rights enshrined in the convention, then it would be a fair balance.[222]

The approach of the United States and United Kingdom does interfere with an individual's right to a private life. Therefore, their approach does not strike a fair balance between the protection of the interests of the community and respect for the rights and freedoms safeguarded by the human rights convention.

The US and UK approaches directly discriminate against a PEP's right to a private life.

4.3 CONCLUSION

This chapter compared the approaches in Nigeria, the United States and United Kingdom with regard to the application of the PEP definition. It has analysed issues that arose from the comparison to determine if there is a need for reform.

Based on the outlined arguments, the United States and the United Kingdom are recommended to extend the application of the PEP definition to individuals who hold prominent public functions within their countries.

This recommended approach would strike a fair balance between the protection of the interests of the community and respect for the rights and freedoms safeguarded by the human rights convention.

---

222 See Belgian Linguistic Case (1979–80) 1 EHRR 252, Para 13.

CHAPTER 5

CASH COURIERS

The Financial Action Task Force (FATF)—an independent intergovernmental body that develops and promotes policies to protect the global financial system against money laundering, terrorist financing and financing the proliferation of weapons of mass destruction—has advised countries to enact laws that require all persons who physically transport currency or bearer negotiable instruments (BNIs) in excess of fifteen thousand US dollars or Euros to submit a truthful declaration to the designated competent authorities.

Countries may opt from among the following three types of declaration systems: (i) a written declaration system for all travellers, (ii) a written declaration system for those travellers carrying an amount of currency or BNIs above the threshold and (iii) an oral declaration system. These systems are described below in their pure forms. However, it is not uncommon for countries to opt for a mixed system.[223]

(a) Written declaration system for all travellers: In this system, all travellers are required to complete a written declaration before entering the country. This would include questions on a common or customs declaration form. In practice, travellers must declare whether or not they are carrying currency or BNIs (e.g., by ticking a yes or no box).[224]

---

223 The Financial Action Task Force (FATF): International Standards on Combating Money Laundering and the financing of terrorism and proliferation, (The FATF Recommendations) 2012, Recommendation 32

224 Ibid.

(b) Written declaration system for travellers carrying amounts above a threshold: In this system, all travellers carrying an amount of currency or BNIs above a preset designated threshold are required to complete a written declaration form. In practice, travellers who are not carrying currency or BNIs over the designated threshold are not required to fill out any forms.[225]

(c) Oral declaration system for all travellers: In this system, all travellers are required to orally declare if they carry an amount of currency or BNIs above a prescribed threshold. This is usually done at customs entry points where travellers are required to choose between the 'red channel' (goods to declare) and the 'green channel' (nothing to declare). The traveller's choice of channel is considered the oral declaration. In practice, travellers do not declare in writing but are required to actively report to a customs official.[226]

While countries have followed the advice of the FATF, the laws in these countries are not identical. For example, Nigeria and the United Kingdom require all travellers to orally declare if they carry an amount of currency above the prescribed threshold, while the United States requires travellers who carry an amount of currency above a preset designated threshold to complete a written declaration form.

This chapter compares the approach adopted by Nigeria and United Kingdom with that of the United States to determine the best approach. This is likely the one that strikes a fair balance between protecting the financial system against money launderers and upholding equality before the law.

---

[225] Ibid.

[226] Ibid.

5.1 DECLARATION SYSTEM

5.1.1 NIGERIA

The dual channel system of passenger clearance is operated at Lagos/Abuja International Airports. By choosing a specifically designated exit, the traveller declares either that he is carrying with him an amount less than ten thousand dollars or an amount equivalent to ten thousand dollars or more than ten thousand dollars.

There are two designated exits and a passenger goes through one of the exits with all his baggage loaded on a trolley: -

5.1.1.1 Green Exit

A passenger who is satisfied that he does not have ten thousand dollars or more is to pass through the green exit indicated by a green regular octagon with the words "NOTHING TO DECLARE" in English or "RIEN A DECLARER" in French.

5.1.1.2 Red Exit

A passenger who has ten thousand dollars or more is to pass through the Red channel indicated by a read square with the words "GOODS TO DECLARE" in English or "MERCHANDISES A DECLARER" IN French and to declare such goods to the Customs officer by the Examination bench.

By choosing a channel, a passenger is, by implication, declaring the contents of his baggage.[227]

[227] Nigeria Customs Service, 'Passenger's Concessions' (https://www.customs.gov.ng) https://www.customs.gov.ng/Stakeholders/passengers_concessions.php Accessed 7th September 2014.

Any person who falsely declares or fails to make a declaration to the Nigerian Custom Service is guilty of an offence and shall be liable on conviction to forfeit the undeclared funds or negotiable instrument or to imprisonment to a term of not less than 2 years or to both.[228]

5.1.2 UNITED STATES

When entering the United States in-transit to a foreign destination, you will be required to clear U.S. Customs Border Protection (CBP) and Immigration and Customs Enforcement. If you have "negotiable monetary instruments" (i.e. currency, personal checks (endorsed), travellers checks, gold coins, securities or stocks in bearer form) valued at ten thousand dollars or more in your possession a "Report of International Transportation of Currency or Monetary Instruments" form FinCEN 105 must be submitted to a CBP Officer upon your entry into the United States.

Monetary instruments that are made payable to a named person but are not endorsed or which bear restrictive endorsements are not subject to reporting requirements, nor are credit cards with credit lines of over ten thousand dollars. Gold bullion is not a monetary instrument for purposes of this requirement. The requirement to report monetary instruments on a FinCEN 105 does not apply to imports of gold bullion.

Failure to declare monetary instruments in amounts of or over ten thousand dollars can result in its seizure.[229]

---

228 Money Laundering Prohibition Act 2011 (as amended), s. 2 (5)

229 U.S Department of Homeland Security, 'Declaring currency when entering the U.S in-transit to a foreign destination' (https://help.cbp.gov) https://help.cbp.gov/app/answers/detail/a_id/778/~/declaring-currency-when-entering-the-u.s.-in-transit-to-a-foreign-destination Accessed 7th September 2014.

5.1.3 UNITED KINGDOM

When you arrive in the United Kingdom, you'll have to go through customs. Most UK ports and airports have three customs exits or 'channels', while some have only one exit, with a red-point phone for declaring goods.

5.1.3.1 When to use the blue channel

You should use the blue channel if you are travelling from a country within the European Union (EU) and you have no banned or restricted goods.

This exit is not seen present in the Nigerian airports. The reason could be that Nigeria does not differentiate between European citizens and other citizens.

5.1.3.2 When to use the green channel

You should use the green channel if you are travelling from outside the EU and have with you less than ten thousand euros (or equivalent) in cash.

Customs officials from the UK Border Agency (UKBA) carry out checks on travellers in the green channel and **there are penalties for failing to declare goods. This can include seizure of: duty free allowance goods, any goods in excess of your duty-free allowance, any vehicle used to transport the goods.**

5.1.3.3 When to use the red channel or red-point phone

You should use the red channel or the red-point phone if you have ten thousand euros or more (or equivalent) in cash.

You'll be able to speak to a UKBA officer either in person or by using the red-point phone. You should tell them everything that you are bringing into the country. The UKBA officer may ask to look inside your luggage.[230]

5.2 DISCUSSION

As stated earlier, Nigeria and the United Kingdom require travellers to orally declare whether they carry an amount of currency above the prescribed threshold, while the United States requires all travellers who carry an amount above a preset designated threshold to complete a written declaration form.

This section determines what the best approach is. The best approach is likely the one that strikes a fair balance between protecting the financial system against money launderers[231] and upholding equality before the law.[232]

5.2.1 PROTECTING THE FINANCIAL SYSTEM AGAINST MONEY LAUNDERERS AND TERRORISTS

The oral declaration system adopted in Nigeria does not appear to be working as effectively as it is in the United Kingdom. This could be because the so-called system has not curtailed the movement of criminal property by the deadly terrorist group Boko Haram.

Boko Haram primarily uses a system of couriers to move cash around Nigeria and across the porous borders from neighbouring

---

230 HM Revenue and Customs, 'Going through customs' (http://www.hmrc.gov.uk) http://www.hmrc.gov.uk/customs/arriving/customs-channels.htm Accessed 7th September 2014.

231 The Financial Action Task Force (FATF): International Standards On Combating Money Laundering and the financing of terrorism and proliferation,(The FATF Recommendations) 2012, Page 9.

232 African Charter on Human and Peoples Rights (1981) Article 2; American Convention on Human Rights (1969) Article 1, 24; European Convention on Human Rights (1950) as amended, Article 14; J. Rehman, *International Human Rights Law,* 2nd edition (Pearson Education Limited, 2010), 214.

African states. This cash is said to be derived from lucrative criminal activities that involve kidnappings.[233]

Nigeria's use of higher denomination bank notes than those of the United Kingdom could be one of the reasons why the oral declaration system does not work as effectively. People are able to move large sums of money around without being detected.

The problem could be solved if the federal government directed the Central Bank of Nigeria (CBN) to stop the production of higher denomination bank notes. This would enable law enforcement agents to identify persons carrying large sums of money.

The written declaration system appears to be working effectively in the United States. So far, there has been little or no record of any terrorist threat from within the United States, apart from the Boston bombings.

5.2.2 UPHOLDING EQUALITY BEFORE THE LAW

This section will determine if the approaches adopted in Nigeria, the United States and the United Kingdom directly violate the human rights of foreign individuals.

It will determine this by looking into the conditions that must be cumulatively met in order for direct discrimination to be considered to have occurred. These conditions include differential treatment, prohibited grounds, lack of objective and reasonable justification and no reasonable relationship of proportionality.[234]

---

233 P. Stewart and L. Wroughton, 'How Boko Haram Is Beating US Efforts to Choke Its Financing' (http://www.reuters.com, July 1, 2014) http://www.reuters.com/article/2014/07/01/us-usa-nigeria-bokoharam-insight-idUSKBN0F636920140701, accessed August 5, 2014.

234 Belgian Linguistic Case (1979–80) 1 EHRR 252, Para 10; Swedish Engine Driver's Union v. Sweden (1979–80) 1 EHRR, 617, Para 45, 47, 48; National Union of Belgian Police v. Belgium (1979–80) 1 EHRR 578, Para 44, 46; Engel and Others v.

5.2.2.1 Differential Treatment

One of the conditions that must exist before a situation is considered direct discrimination is that there must be a given difference in treatment that may concern the exercise of any right set forth by law.[235]

The Nigerian approach does create a difference in treatment, as it operates the dual-channel system of passenger clearance. This requires travellers who are carrying amounts of less than ten thousand dollars to go through the green channel exit, while passengers with amounts equivalent to ten thousand dollars or more must go through the red channel exit.

The United Kingdom's approach does create a difference in treatment concerning the exercise of certain rights set forth by law. This is because European Union passengers are required to go through the blue channel, while other passengers choose either the green or red channel, depending on the amount of cash they are carrying.

Both Nigeria and the United Kingdom's approaches could interfere with a person's right to privacy, such as when a passenger going through the red channel is forced to reveal confidential information to airport staff. This information can include source of income and source of wealth.

The US approach does create a difference in treatment, as it requires passengers who are carrying amounts over ten thousand dollars to submit a Form FinCEN 105, Report of International Transportation of Currency or Monetary Instruments, to a customs and border patrol officer, while travellers carrying less

---

The Netherlands (No.1) (1979–80) 1 EHRR 647, Para 72; The Republic of Ireland v. The United Kingdom (1979–80) 2 EHRR 25, Para 226.

235 Belgian Linguistic Case (1979–80) 1 EHRR 252, Para 10; National Union of Belgian Police v. Belgium (1979–80) 1 EHRR 578 Para 44, 46.

than ten thousand dollars are not required to submit any such form.

Just like the UK and Nigerian approaches, the US approach could interfere with a person's right to privacy. This can occur when a person filling out Form FinCEN 105 is forced to reveal confidential information to the officer in charge. This information includes source of wealth and source of income.

5.2.2.2 Prohibited Grounds

The respective human rights conventions provide that discrimination could be on the grounds of sex, race, colour, national or social origin, property, birth or other status.[236]

The Nigerian, US and UK approaches do discriminate on the grounds of currency.

5.2.2.3 Without Objective and Reasonable Justification

The third condition for direct discrimination is that the distinction or difference in treatment would have no objective and reasonable justification. The existence of such a justification must be assessed in relation to the aim and effects of the measure under consideration.[237] This means that the aims and objectives of the Nigerian, UK and US approaches must be looked at to determine if they have no reasonable justification.

The aim and objective of the measure in all three countries is to prevent physical cross-border transportation of illegal money.

---

236 African Charter on Human and Peoples Rights (1981) Article 2; American Convention on Human Rights, Article 1; European Convention on Human Rights (1950) as amended, Article 14.

237 Belgian Linguistic Case (1979–80) 1 EHRR 252, Para 10; National Union of Belgian Police v. Belgium (1979–80) 1 EHRR 578, Para 46.

Persons carrying criminal property into Nigeria and the United Kingdom would be detected at the red channel, while persons carrying criminal property into the United States would be detected once the information provided in Form FinCEN 105 was verified. This justifies the Nigerian and US human rights interference.

The United Kingdom is justified to the extent of its utilization of the green and red channels. The blue channel, however, directly discriminates against citizens who are not Europeans, since the channel is not designed to prevent physical cross-border transportation of illegal money.

There is no need to further determine whether or not the Nigerian, US and UK approaches meet the other direct discrimination requirements.

5.3 CONCLUSION

In view of these arguments, the following are recommended:

I. The United Kingdom should adopt the Nigerian approach by operating only the green and red channels.

II. The Nigerian National Assembly should pass a law prohibiting every person from physically carrying more than fifty thousand Nigerian naira. This measure would force people, including cash couriers, to use their debit and credit cards more often, making it easier for banks to monitor financial transactions and report suspicious activities.

CHAPTER 6

COMPLIANCE OFFICERS

The Financial Action Task Force (FATF) has advised countries to enact laws that require financial institutions to implement programmes against money laundering and terrorist financing. These programmes should include the appointment of a compliance officer at the management level.[238]

A compliance officer is responsible for the oversight of the firm's anti–money laundering (AML) systems and controls, which include appropriate training for the firm's employees in relation to money laundering and considering each report received from staff to determine whether it gives rise to knowledge, suspicion or reasonable grounds for knowledge or suspicion that another person is engaged in money laundering.[239]

Although countries have followed the advice of the FATF, the enacted laws are not identical. For example, Nigeria and the United States require financial institutions to appoint compliance officers who receive disclosures from staff and who train staff.[240] The United Kingdom requires financial institutions to appoint

---

238 The Financial Action Task Force (FATF): International Standards on Combating Money Laundering and the financing of terrorism and proliferation, (The FATF Recommendations) 2012, Recommendation 18

239 Money Laundering Prohibition Act 2011 (as amended), s 9 (1); Federal Financial Institutions Examination Council, *Bank Secrecy Act/Anti–Money Laundering Examination Manual (2010)*, 36; Senior Management Arrangements, Systems and Controls (SYSC), 6.3.9 (1) R, see also SYSC, 6.3.7 G.

240 Money Laundering Prohibition Act 2011 (as amended), s 9 (1); Federal Financial Institutions Examination Council, *Bank Secrecy Act/Anti–Money Laundering Examination Manual* (2010), 36.

compliance officers with the responsibility of training staff,[241] but the duty of receiving disclosures from staff rests on the nominated officer.[242]

This chapter compares the approach adopted in Nigeria and the United States with that of the United Kingdom, with the aim of determining if Nigeria and the United States should adopt the approach of the United Kingdom or if there is no need for reform.

The comparison will be made under two subheadings: 'The Title of the Individual Responsible for Anti–Money Laundering Compliance' and 'Duties and Responsibilities'.

The chapter will later analyse issues that arise from the comparison to determine if there is need for reform.

6.1 THE TITLE OF THE INDIVIDUAL RESPONSIBLE FOR ANTI MONEY LAUNDERING COMPLIANCE

6.1.1 NIGERIA

The individual responsible for coordinating and monitoring day-to-day Anti Money Laundering compliance is known as the compliance officer.[243]

6.1.2 UNITED STATES

The individual responsible for coordinating and monitoring day-to-day Anti Money Laundering compliance is known as the compliance officer.[244]

---

241 Senior Management Arrangements, Systems and Controls (SYSC), 6.3.9 (1) R, see also SYSC, 6.3.7 G.

242 Proceeds of Crime Act 2002 (as amended), ss. 337, 338; Money Laundering Regulations (2007), Regulation 20 (2) (d) (i). See Regulation 3 (1) for the list of firms in the regulated sector.

243 Money Laundering Prohibition Act 2011 (as amended), s. 9 (1) (a)

6.1.3 UNITED KINGDOM

The individual responsible for coordinating and monitoring day-to-day Anti Money Laundering compliance is known as the money laundering reporting officer.[245]

The title given to such individual appears to be different from that of the FATF.

6.2 DUTIES AND RESPONSIBLITIES

6.2.1 NIGERIA

Compliance officers are under a duty: to receive disclosures from staffs in the firm and to train staffs in the firm.[246]

6.2.2 UNITED STATES

Compliance officers are under a duty: to receive disclosures from staffs in the firm and to train staffs in the firm.[247]

6.2.3 UNITED KINGDOM

Compliance officers are under a duty to train staffs in the firm.[248] The duty to receive disclosures from staffs in the firm rests on the Nominated Officer.[249]

In practice, the compliance officer and nominated officer will be one and the same person.[250]

---

244 Federal Financial Institutions Examination Council: Bank Secrecy Act/Anti-Money Laundering Examination Manual 2010, Page 36

245 Senior Management Arrangements, Systems and Controls (SYSC), 6.3.9 (1) R, see also SYSC, 6.3.7 G

246 Money Laundering Prohibition Act 2011 (as amended), s. 9 (1)

247 Federal Financial Institutions Examination Council: Bank Secrecy Act/Anti-Money Laundering Examination Manual 2010, Page 36

248 Senior Management Arrangements, Systems and Controls (SYSC), 6.3.9 (1) R, see also SYSC, 6.3.7 G

249 Money Laundering Regulations 2007, Regulation 20 (2) (d) (i), See also Regulation 3 (1) for list of firms in the regulated sector.

6.3 DISCUSSION

The previous section compared the approach in Nigeria with that in the United States and the United Kingdom as it relates to compliance officers. This section will analyse issues that arose to determine if there is a need for reform.

6.3.1 DUTIES AND RESPONSIBILITIES

As stated earlier, the duties of compliance officers in Nigeria and the United States include receiving disclosures from staff and training staff, while compliance officers in the United Kingdom train staff, but receiving disclosures from staff is the responsibility of the nominated officer.

This section will determine if Nigeria and the United States need to adopt the approach used in the United Kingdom, or if there is no need for reform.

The United Kingdom's approach allows for the responsibilities conferred on compliance officers by the FATF to be shared between two people, thereby reducing the burden of work on the compliance officers. This is not the approach adopted by Nigeria and the United States.

However, compliance officers in Nigeria and the United States could delegate some of their duties to other competent individuals.[251]

---

[250] The Joint Money Laundering Steering Group JMLSG, Prevention of money laundering/combating terrorist financing 2013 Revised Version, Guidance for the UK financial sector Part I, Amended November 2013, Paragraph 3.4

[251] Federal Financial Institutions Examination Council, *Bank Secrecy Act/Anti–Money Laundering Examination Manual* (2010), 36.

6.4 CONCLUSION

This chapter compared the approach in Nigeria with that of the United States and the United Kingdom as it relates to compliance officers. It also analysed issues that arose from the comparison to determine that the Nigerian and US money laundering laws do not need to adopt the approach of the United Kingdom.

CHAPTER 7

THE OFFENCE OF BRIBERY

The Financial Action Task Force (FATF) has advised countries to apply the crime of money laundering to all serious offences, with a view of including the widest range of predicate offences.[252]

A predicate offence is any offence that generates proceeds that may become the subject of an offence of money laundering.[253] They include the offences of bribery and corruption.[254]

Bribery can be defined as the promising, offering or giving to a public official, directly or indirectly, an undue advantage for the official, or another person or entity, in order to cause that official to act or refrain from acting in the exercise of official duties.[255]

This chapter starts by briefly highlighting the relevant bribery laws and regulations in Nigeria, the United States and the United Kingdom. Then it will compare the bribery laws in the United Kingdom with those of the United States and Nigeria.

The comparison will be done under three subheadings: 'Strict Liability', 'Extraterritorial Jurisdiction' and 'Penalties'.

---

252 The Financial Action Task Force (FATF): International Standards on Combating Money Laundering and the Financing of Terrorism and Proliferation, (The FATF Recommendations) 2012, Interpretive Note to Recommendation 3

253 United Nations Convention against Transnational Organized Crime and the Protocol Thereto (2004), Article 2 (h).

254 United Nations Convention against Transnational Organized Crime and the Protocol Thereto (2004), Article 8.

255 United Nations Convention against Transnational Organized Crime and the Protocol Thereto (2004), Article 8 (1) (a).

7.1 RELEVANT BRIBERY LAWS AND REGULATIONS

7.1.1 UNITED KINGDOM

The law enacted to combat bribery and corruption in the United Kingdom is the Bribery Act 2010.

7.1.2 UNITED STATES

The law enacted to combat bribery and corruption in the Unites States is the Foreign Corrupt Practices Act 1977 (as amended).

7.1.3 NIGERIA

The laws enacted to combat bribery and corruption in Nigeria include Criminal Code Act and the Corrupt Practices and Other Related Offences Act 2000.

7.2 STRICT LIABILITY

The United Kingdom Bribery Act makes it a strict liability offence for a company to fail to prevent bribery. This proviso is not present in the Nigerian and US bribery laws.[256]

The strict liability offence of failing to prevent bribery does not require knowledge, intention or recklessness. All it requires is that a person associated with the commercial organization acted on behalf of that organization with the intention of retaining a business or an advantage for the organization.[257]

What this means is that if someone were instructed by a company to negotiate business on its behalf, and that person paid a bribe to the individual or company being negotiated with without being told to do so and the company did not have adequate procedures

[256] Corrupt Practices and Other Related Offences Act (2000), s 8, 9; Foreign Corrupt Practices Act (1977), 15 USC, s 78 dd-1 (a).
[257] Bribery Act 2010 s 7 (1).

in place, the company would be liable for failing to prevent bribery—even if the person who paid the bribe failed to reveal the deed to the company. This would definitely offend the principle governing the agency and principal relationship, which requires that an agent must act on the instructions of the principal and if he does not do so he is acting on his own behalf.[258] It could also offend the principle of vicarious liability if such a person were not an employee.[259]

This will likely have a serious impact on commercial insurance broker firms that are regulated by the Financial Conduct Authority (FCA), which was formally the Financial Services Authority (FSA).[260] The FCA released a report with regard to its visits to seventeen broker firms, which confirmed that commercial insurance broker firms could not demonstrate that adequate procedures were in place to prevent bribery.[261] This means that if a bribe were committed by a third party in a commercial insurance broker firm, three parties would likely be affected: the broker firm, the parent company (if it's a subsidiary to one) and the firm it acts for. Let's take, for example, the case between the FSA and Aon Limited (an insurance broker/intermediary). In January 2009, Aon Limited was fined five million, two hundred and fifty thousand pounds by the FSA for failures in its antibribery systems and controls. The firm was said to have made suspicious payments totalling seven million

---

[258] C. Elliott and F. Quinn, *Contract Law,* 7th edition (Pearson Education Limited, 2009), 279 for the principles governing Agency/Principal Relationship.
[259] K. Horsey and E. Rackley, *Tort Law,* 2nd edition (Oxford University Press, 2011), 328. States that an employer can only be liable for acts of employees and the Bribery Act extends this to anyone acting on its behalf. See also R. Kidner, *Casebook on Torts,* 12th edition (Oxford University Press, 2012), 217–218.
[260] P. Yeoh, *Bribery Act 2010: Implications for Regulated Firms* (Legislative Comment) 2012 20 (3), JFR and C, 264–277 for details on the new status of the Financial Services Authority (FSA).
[261] Financial Crime: A Guide for Firms, Part 2: A Firm's Guide to Preventing Financial Crime by the Financial Conduct Authority April 2013.

pounds to overseas firms and individuals who helped generate business in higher-risk jurisdictions. No due diligence was carried out, the company did not have a risk-based system and the company failed to train its staff on bribery.[262]

Based on the new offence of 'failure to prevent' in the UK Bribery Act, in addition to the fine imposed by the FCA, the company would also be fined under the Bribery Act. The fine could be justified, since the company deliberately did not do any due diligence on the third parties and this has given other firms the opportunity to compete in the market. What may not be justified is that the parent company of Aon Limited, Aon Corporation,[263] could also be fined under the Bribery Act for failing to prevent Aon Limited from committing bribery if the prosecutors were able to establish that Aon Limited was acting on behalf of Aon Corporation. This could be even worse if Aon Limited told the authorities that they were acting on behalf of the parent company when, in actual fact, they were not.

Another party that could be affected is the principal Aon Limited actually worked for, since Aon Limited is an insurance broker. If the principal is a firm, then it could face the same challenges as Aon Corporation.

This law could be regarded as good in a situation where Aon Corporation had knowledge that Aon Limited was acting on its behalf, or it could be good if the principal Aon Limited acted for knew that Aon was acting on its behalf. What may not be good is if neither party had any knowledge whatsoever of the bribery. This is even the case when neither party had control over the

---

262 Ibid.

263 Aon Plc (2013), http://www.aon.com/about-aon/about-aon.jsp, Accessed on May 20, 2013.

other. This, on its own, not only offends the agency and principal relationship, but the principle of vicarious liability.

Another case was between the FSA and Willis Limited. Willis was also an insurance broker and was fined for not having antibribery systems and controls in place to prevent bribery.[264] Willis's parent company (Willis Group Holdings)[265] could share the same fate as Aon Corporation. An interesting discovery was that Willis Limited is a Lloyds broker.[266] If action was brought under the Bribery Act, Lloyds could be indicted for failing to prevent bribery. This would be unjustified if Lloyds did not know anything.

In the unregulated sector, the impact will likely be higher, based on the fact that the majority of people working for the company could be trying to win contracts for the company, as seen in SEC v. Lucent Technologies Inc., Case No 07-cv-2301 (DDC 21 Dec 2007) ECF no 1 and other similar cases, and the company may not be able to prevent it.[267] If a third party were to bribe someone on the company's behalf, two parties will likely be affected: the subsidiary and the parent companies.

---

264 Financial Crime: a guide for firms Part 1: A firm's guide to preventing financial crime by the Financial Conduct Authority April 2013.

265 Willis Limited (2013), http://www.willis.com/Regulation/, accessed May 15, 2013.

266 Ibid.

267 See SEC v. Alcatel-Lucent, SA Case No 10–cv–24620 (SD Fla Dec 27 2010) ECF No. 1, see SEC v. ABB LTD, Case No 10, 10-cv-1648, (DDC Sep 29 2009) ECF No 1; SEC v. RAE Sys Inc Case No 10-Cv-2093 (DDC Dec 10 2010) ECF No 1; SEC v. ABB Ltd, Case No 4-cv-1141 (DDC July 6 2004) ECF No.1; SEC v. UTS Starcom Inc No 09-cv-6094 (ND Cal Dec 31 2009) ECF No 1; SEC v. Schering–Plough Corp No 4-cv-945 (DDC June 9 2004) ECF No 1; SEC v. Innospec Inc, No 10-cv-448 (DDC March 18 2010) ECF No 1; SEC v. Technip No 10-cv-2289. (SD Tex June 28 2010) ECF No 1; United States v. JGC Corp No 11-cv-260 (SD Tex Apr 6 2011) ECF No 1. See also Growing Beyond: A Place for Integrity 12th Global Survey by Ernst and Young whose survey revealed that 15 percent versus 9 percent employees would like to commit bribery to win business.

Take, for example, the KBR/Halliburton scandal.[268] Stanley, then the CEO of KBR, paid bribes on the company's behalf to secure contracts from Nigeria. KBR was charged under the antibribery provisions of the Foreign Corrupt Practices Act (FCPA), and Halliburton was only charged under the accounting provisions. Although the SEC did not give its reasons for withholding this charge, some writers have argued that Halliburton was not charged under the antibribery provisions because it had no knowledge of what went down, and the FCPA requires that such knowledge be established.[269] This can be supported by the fact that Stanley was asked by senior officials in Halliburton about the money, and Stanley failed to disclose that it was paying bribes on its behalf.

If such a situation were to happen under the Bribery Act, Halliburton would definitely be charged under the antibribery provisions. The question is: Would it be right for the Serious Fraud Office (SFO)[270] to charge Halliburton? One could argue, based on the fact that Halliburton did take efforts to mitigate the risk by conducting due diligence on the UK agent, that it wouldn't be legitimate for the SFO to fine them. But a now-retired senior Halliburton legal officer said that Halliburton approved the use of the agent, despite the fact that the investigation had failed to learn significant information about it. Because Halliburton also did not do due diligence on the Japanese agent, one can confidently say that the United Kingdom would be right to charge Halliburton.

---

[268] SEC v. Halliburton Company and KBR INC Civil Action, 4:09–399.

[269] R. L. Cassin, *'Understanding the KBR Halliburton Charges'* (The FCPA Blog, February 24, 2009), http://fcpablog.squarespace.com/blog/2009/2/24/understanding-the-kbr-halliburton-charges.html, accessed May 16, 2013.

[270] The Joint Prosecution Guidance of the Director of the Serious Fraud Office (SFO) and the Director of Public Prosecutions states that the SFO is the lead agency for the prosecution of overseas corruption (this includes bribery), which is a part of it.

A similar situation happened in SEC v. Magyar Telekom Plc and Deutsche Telekom AG.[271] In that case, Deutsche Telekom, the parent company to Magyar, was in charge of the due-diligence procedure but failed to prevent bribery. In such a case, it would be right for the SFO to charge them.

It would have been a different case if KBR was an indirect subsidiary to Halliburton and Halliburton knew nothing about the use of the UK and Japanese agents, even though its policy governed the use of its agents. This can be seen in the case of SEC v. ENI, SPA and Snamprogetti Netherlands,[272] where Snamprogetti was an indirect subsidiary to ENI. Although ENI's policy governed Snamprogetti's use of agents, it had no idea that Snamprogetti was using those particular agents for the transaction, and it was not the one in charge of doing due diligence. In such a situation, it wouldn't be right for the SFO to charge Halliburton. But in a situation where the parent company had active control over its subsidiary, knew that the subsidiary used a particular agent for a particular transaction, and was in charge of doing due diligence for those agents, then it would be right for the SFO to charge that company.

7.3 EXTRATERRITORIAL JURISDICTION

As stated earlier, it is an offence under Section 7 (1) of the UK Bribery Act for a relevant commercial organization to fail to prevent bribery.[273] However, Section 7 (5) (b) and (d) defines a commercial organization as a body corporate that carries on business or part of its business in the United Kingdom.[274] This

[271] SEC v. Magyar Telekom Plc and Deutsche Telekom AG Case No 11-cv-9646 (S.D.N.Y Dec 29 2011) ECF No 1.
[272] SEC v. ENI S.P.A and Snamprogetti Netherlands BV Case No 10-cv-2414.
[273] Bribery Act 2010, s. 7 (1).
[274] Bribery Act 2010, s. 7 (5) b and d.

means that, provided the organization is incorporated or formed in the United Kingdom or the organization carries on a business or part of a business in the United Kingdom—wherever in the world it may be incorporated or formed—then UK courts will have jurisdiction to prosecute that company whether an offence is committed in the United Kingdom or elsewhere.

This would mean that if a company that carries on business in the United Kingdom operates in another country, and the law of that country allows for the bribery of an official in accordance with business practices or customs, the foreign company would not be subject to such domestic law based on the fact that it carries on business in the United Kingdom. For example, Korean law permits the bribery of an official where such a bribe is done in accordance with accepted business practices.[275] This means that a Korean company doing business in Cambodia that carried on business two years ago in the United Kingdom and that plans to return to the United Kingdom when there are favourable conditions might be liable for the offence of bribery where an agent of the Korean company bribes an agent of the Cambodian company. This is because Section 7 of the UK Bribery Act extends to bribery of officials and not just foreign officials.[276]

Another example could be where a Cambodian company gave an expensive gift to a company situated in Korea in accordance with a particular custom and tradition. Under the new Cambodian anticorruption law, gifts are allowed to be given to officials in accordance with custom and tradition.[277] While the Cambodian company would not have been liable if it never carried on

[275]Republic of Korea Criminal Act, No. 293, Sep 18 1953 as last amended by Act No 10259 April 15 2010, Article 20, Article 133.
[276] Bribery Act 2010, s. 7 (3).
[277] *The Criminalisation of Bribery in Asia and the Pacific: Frameworks and Practices in 28 Asian and Pacific Jurisdictions.* Thematic Review—Final Report by ADB/OECD Anti-Corruption Initiative for Asia and the Pacific 2010.

business in the United Kingdom, it would be liable if it did carry on business there. This provision could infringe on principles of comity.[278]

The same could be said when the law of another country allows an extent of bribery when certain payments are made to foreign officials. The most common is facilitation payments.[279] While the United Kingdom does not allow for facilitation payments, the United States, Australia and Korea do to some extent.[280] The antibribery law of the United States contains a narrow exception for 'facilitation payments' made in furtherance of routine governmental actions. The exception only applies when a payment is made to further 'routine governmental action' that involves nondiscretionary acts.[281] Examples include processing visas.[282] This means that if a US company that carries on business in the United Kingdom were to do business in places such as South Africa, Malawi, Congo, Mozambique, Zambia and Zimbabwe where surveys show that facilitation payments are paid at a high level because foreign officials are highly corrupt,[283] then the US company could not make such payment even to process a visa. If the company did make such a payment, it would be prosecuted by the SFO. The same can be said for companies that

---

278 Paul Marshall, *Part 7 of the Proceeds of Crime Act 2002: Double Criminality, Legal Certainty, Proportionality and Trouble Ahead.* 2003 11 (2) JFC 111–126.

279 See Bribery Act 2010: Joint Prosecution Guidance of the Director of the Serious Fraud Office and the Director of Public Prosecutions, which defines facilitation payments as unofficial payments made to public officials to secure or expedite the performance of a routine governmental action.

280 Foreign Corrupt Practices Act of 1977 (FCPA) 15 USC, s. 78dd-2(b); Australia's Criminal Code Act 1995, s. 70 (4); The Act on Preventing Bribery of Foreign Public Officials in International Business Transactions (FBPA) 1998, Article 3 (2) (b).

281 Foreign Corrupt Practices Act of 1977 (FCPA) 15 USC, s. 78dd-2 (b).

282 *FCPA: A Resource Guide to the US Foreign Corrupt Practices Act* by the Criminal Division of the US Department of Justice and the Enforcement Division of the US Securities and Exchange Commission, November 14, 2012.

283 *Daily Lives and Corruption: Public Opinion in Southern Africa* by Transparency International 2011.

are incorporated in Australia or Korea where the bribery laws allow for small facilitation payments to an extent.[284] It means that companies operating there cannot make such facilitation payments.

The same could be said of laws that allow for bribery of a foreign official where it is in accordance with business practices. This can be seen in Korean law.[285] If someone in a company that is organized under the laws of Korea pays a foreign official money in China to improve the personal relationship for business purposes, this act could lead to an offence under the UK law. This is wrong because, in China, the value of personal relationships and the concept of *guanxi* are the focal points of business culture. *Guanxi* is best described as a personal connection between two people and is typically established by providing personal favours such as gifts, entertainment and other benefits.[286] There is no way that the agent of the Korean company would have known that the United Kingdom would see such a payment as a bribe.

This provision seems to go beyond the scope of the Organization for Economic Co-operation and Development (OECD) convention, which requires its parties to cover foreign bribery committed partly in their own territories.[287] Not only does the

---

284 Australia's Criminal Code Act 1995, s 70 (4); FBPA: The Act on Preventing Bribery of Foreign Public Officials in International Business Transactions (1998), Article 3 (2) (b).

285 FBPA: The Act on Preventing Bribery of Foreign Public Officials in International Business Transactions (1998), Article 3 (1) makes it an offence to bribe a foreign officer, while the Republic of Korea Criminal Act, No 293, Sep 18 1953 as last amended by Act No 10259 April 15, 2010, Article 20, allows for an exception where business practices accept such bribes.

286 Hebert Smith Asia's anticorruption report, issue 1, Summer 2012

287 OECD Convention on Combating Bribery of Foreign Officials in International Business Transactions (1997), Article 4 (1). See also United Nations Convention against Corruption 2004, Article 42 (1), which does not cover the type of jurisdiction the United Kingdom is using. See also the Nigerian Criminal Code Act 2004, s. 12,

United Kingdom extend its jurisdiction of foreign bribery over acts that are not committed in the United Kingdom, it even exercises jurisdiction over commercial bribery.[288] This goes further than the United States. The FCPA applies to SEC issuers (US and foreign companies),[289] domestic concerns[290] and certain foreign nationals or entities that act within the United States.[291]

Such broad provisions made Jessica A. Lordi ask the question: Is this extraterritorial provision even legal under international law? Lordi argues that if the United Kingdom uses this provision as a means of prosecuting bribery anywhere in the world against companies with any level of connection to the United Kingdom, the law could reach permissible extraterritorial jurisdiction and effectively establish universal jurisdiction for bribery offences. According to Lordi, the United Kingdom should not use such jurisdiction as it is often used for egregious acts, piracy, war crimes, genocide and terrorism. Bribery is not as serious as these offences. She also argues that various countries have amended and updated their antibribery laws, but none reach the level of prosecutorial discretion or extraterritorial reach that the Bribery Act employs. Lastly, she argues that since bribery is widely defined, it would be wrong to apply universal jurisdiction to it. Universal jurisdiction applies when the crime is universally identified, and there is no need for the United Kingdom to

---

which implements Article 4 (1) of the OECD Convention. F. Nwadialo S.A.N, The *Criminal Procedure of the Southern States of Nigeria,* 2nd edition (MIJ Professional Publishers Limited, 1987) 14–15.

288 Bribery Act 2010, s. 1.

289 Foreign Corrupt Practices Act (1977), 15 USC, s. 78 dd-1; Securities Exchange Act (1934)1, Section 30 A.

290 Foreign Corrupt Practices Act (1977), 15 USC, s. 78 dd-2.

291 Ibid.

operate on behalf of the international community to prosecute bribery.[292]

While the definition of bribery may be too wide to fit into the universal jurisdiction principle, bribery is arguably as serious as war crimes and piracy, and universal jurisdiction could be used. Bribery, which is a part of corruption, is an insidious plague that has a wide range of corrosive effects on societies. It undermines democracy and the rule of law and leads to violations of human rights.[293] If this were the only criteria, the SFO would be justified in using universal jurisdiction. However, since it does offend the customs of others, leads to confusion and has a negative impact on business, universal jurisdiction should not be used.

7.4 PENALTIES

The UK bribery law is such that if a company is convicted of failing to prevent bribery, it will be liable, upon indictment, to an unlimited fine.[294]

Nigeria and the United States, on the other hand, impose a limit on the penalty.[295]

It is unclear what method the courts in the United Kingdom intend to use to calculate the penalty. This definitely leads to a lot of uncertainty in that regard. The reason the exact amount is not

[292] J. A. Lordi, *The United Kingdom Bribery Act: Endless Jurisdictional Liability on Corporate Violators* 2012 Vol 44 Case W Res J Int LL, 955; M. D. Evans, *International Law,* 3rd edition (Oxford University Press, 2010), 326–327. This also emphasises the fact that universal jurisdiction is applied to serious crimes like war crimes and piracy. R. K. Gardiner, *International Law,* first published (Pearson Education Ltd, 2003), 312. Describes the *universal principle* as determining jurisdiction by reference to the place where the offence was committed.

[293] United Nations Convention against Corruption 2004 (Foreword).

[294] Bribery Act 2010, s. 11(3).

[295] Corrupt Practices and Other Related Offences Act 2000, s 17; Foreign Corrupt Practices Act of 1977 (FCPA) 15 USC, s. 78dd-2 (g).

specified may be that the scope of the Bribery Act is much wider than the FCPA, and it wouldn't be fair to impose the same penalty on a company where the agent bribed an official as on a company where the agent bribed a foreign official. While this may be a creative approach, the courts may still end up doing what they sought to avoid. The courts are likely to interpret cases differently and, therefore, could impose a serious penalty on one company, and then impose a lesser penalty on another, even when the facts of the cases are similar. This could even conflict with Article 3 (1) of the OECD Convention, which requires that such sanctions should be proportionate.[296] If the court is able to treat everyone fairly, then there may be no issue.

7.5 CONCLUSION

We have seen that Section 7 of the UK Bribery Act can cause many issues for firms, both in the regulated and unregulated sectors. Firms with no knowledge of an act can pay unwarranted fines. Also the extraterritorial reach of the act conflicts with other countries' domestic and foreign laws, making it illegal to an extent. One can confidently say that there is need for reform.

Cecilia Wells has suggested that Section 7 be amended to allow for vicarious liability with a due-diligence defence,[297] while the Law Commission suggested that the act allow for negligence in failing to prevent bribery, subject to adequate procedures.[298] Wells's suggestion is recommended, along with an amendment to the definition of associated persons to restrict it to companies incorporated under UK law.

[296] OECD Convention Article 3 (1).

[297] C. Wells, *'Bribery: corporate liability under the draft bill 2009'.* (2009) 7, Criminal Law Review, 479–487.

[298] The Law Commission (LAW Com No 313) Reforming Bribery (2008) Paragraph 6.1.

With regard to whether facilitation payments should remain prohibited, some have argued against distinguishing between a facilitation payment and a bribe, while others have argued that facilitation payments should be allowed on the basis that they may be solicited under threat, making refusal difficult.[299] Facilitation payments should not be prohibited due to uncertainty, and should be made a defence, as long as it is not wide enough to create uncertainty. The United Kingdom could adopt the approach of the United States by limiting facilitation payments to routine governmental actions.

---

[299] R. Drinnan, *'Australia: proposed reform to Australian foreign bribery legislation'* (2012), 2, IELR, 40–42.

CHAPTER 8

PLEA BARGAINING

The Financial Action Task Force (FATF) has advised countries to adopt measures that enable their competent authorities to freeze or seize and confiscate laundered property.[300] These measures include the introduction of the concept of plea bargaining into a country's criminal justice system. This measure ensures that all criminal proceeds are confiscated.

In a plea bargain deal, both sides gain something from the arrangement. The prosecution gains a conviction without the time and expense of a trial, while the defendant might get a reduced sentence or have some of the charges dropped. In some cases, for example, the prosecution will offer a plea deal so that the victim does not have to go through the drama and stress of testifying at a trial.[301]

While countries have adopted the concept of plea bargaining into their criminal justice system, the application of the concept in these countries is not identical.

This chapter seeks to compare the approach in Nigeria with those of the United States and the United Kingdom to determine the best approach. This is likely the one that achieves the highest

---

[300] The Financial Action Task Force (FATF): International Standards on Combating Money Laundering and the Financing of Terrorism and Proliferation, (The FATF Recommendations) 2012, Interpretive Note to Recommendation 4

[301] C. Montaldo, *'The plea bargain stage of a criminal case, stages of the criminal justice system'* (http://crime.about.com) http://crime.about.com/od/Crime_101/a/The-Plea-Bargain-Stage-Of-A-Criminal-Case.htm, accessed July 4, 2014.

number of convictions without necessarily interfering with a person's right to a jury trial.[302]

This chapter will start by defining what plea bargaining is and giving a brief introduction of the history and nature of plea bargaining. Then it will compare the approach adopted in Nigeria with those of the United States and the United Kingdom.

8.1 DEFINITION OF PLEA BARGAINING

To a layman on the street, plea bargaining in the Nigerian context is a system in which room is provided for unfettered looting of public treasury at all levels of governance in our country. This is done in such a way that billions of naira is stolen, and some paltry millions are returned to the coffers of the government, while a large chunk of the looted public funds at the end of the day is left for the looter and his/her unborn generations.[303]

But to an Advocate of Legal Practice, plea bargaining consists of the exchange of official concessions for a defendant's act of self-conviction. These concessions may relate to the sentence imposed by the Court or recommended by the prosecution, the offence charged, or a variety of other circumstances; they may be explicit or implicit; and they may proceed from any of a number of officials.[304] The benefit offered by the defendant, however is always the same: entry of[305] a plea of guilty. This definition excludes unilateral exercises of prosecutorial or judicial discretion, such as an unqualified dismissal or reduction of charges. It also

[302] Note that a judge can only make a confiscation order after a conviction has been secured.
[303] O Joseph, *'Why encourage plea bargaining?'* (http://www.punchng.com, 2nd September 2012) http://www.punchng.com/opinion/letters/why-encourage-plea-bargaining/ Accessed 3rd July 2014.
[304] A Alschuler, *'Plea Bargaining and its History'* 1979, 79 Columbia Law Review 1, 3.
[305] Ibid

excludes the exchange of official concessions for actions other than entry of a guilty plea, such as offering restitution to the victim of a crime, giving information or testimony concerning other alleged offenders, or resigning from public office following allegations of misconduct.[306]

Black's Law Dictionary defines plea bargain as follows:

A negotiated agreement between a prosecutor and a criminal defendant whereby the defendant pleads guilty to a lesser offence or to one of multiple charges in exchange for some concession by the prosecutor[307]

8.2 HISTORY OF PLEA BARGAINING

The plea bargain was a prosecutorial tool used only episodically before the 19th century. "In America," Fisher says, "it can be traced almost to the very emergence of public prosecution -- and public prosecution, although not exclusive to the United States., developed earlier and more broadly in the United States than in most places."

Below is a summary of the history of plea bargaining from the 16th century to the 19th century

1633: Galileo gets house arrest from the Inquisition in exchange for his reciting penitential psalms weekly and recanting Copernican heresies.

1931: Al Capone brags about his light sentence for pleading guilty to tax evasion and Prohibition violations. The judge then declares that he isn't bound by the bargain, and Capone does seven and a half years in Alcatraz.

---

306 A Alschuler, '*Plea Bargaining and its History*' 1979, 79 Columbia Law Review 1, 4.
307 B A. Garner, *Black's Law Dictionary* (8th Edition West, a Thomson business 2004) 1190.

1969: To avoid execution, James Earl Ray pleads guilty to assassinating Martin Luther King Jr. and gets 99 years.

1973: Spiro Agnew resigns the vice presidency and pleads no contest to the charge of failing to report income; he gets three years' probation and a ten thousand dollars fine (roughly one-third of the amount at issue).

1990: Facing serious federal charges of insider trading, Michael Milken pleads to lesser charges of securities fraud; soon after, his 10-year sentence is reduced to 2 years.[308]

8.3 THE NATURE OF PLEA BARGAINING

There are two basic types of plea bargaining: charge bargain and sentence bargain. In the case of charge bargain, it is arranged in a way that the prosecutor agrees to drop some of the counts or reduce the charge to a less serious offence in exchange for a plea of either guilty or no contest from the defendant.

In the case of sentence bargain, the prosecutor agrees to recommend a lighter sentence in exchange for a plea of either guilty or no contest from the defendant.[309]

8.4 DISCUSSION

The previous sections defined plea bargaining and discussed the history and nature of plea bargaining.

This section compares the approach to plea bargaining in Nigeria with those of the United States and the United Kingdom. The

---

[308] D Olin, '*The Way We Live Now: 9-29-02: Crash Course; Plea Bargain*' (http://www.nytimes.com 29th September 2002) http://www.nytimes.com/2002/09/29/magazine/the-way-we-live-now-9-29-02-crash-course-plea-bargain.html Accessed 3rd July 2014.

[309] B A. Garner, *Black's Law Dictionary* (8th Edition West, a Thomson business 2004) 1190.

aim of this comparison is to determine what the best approach is, which is the one that achieves the highest number of convictions without necessarily interfering with a person's right to a jury trial.

8.4.1 NIGERIA

The practice of plea bargaining is obviously very embryonic in Nigeria. It was never part of any Nigerian law until 2002 when the **Economic and Financial Crimes Commission (the Commission)** was established. Looking at a plethora of statutory provisions in Nigeria, the author has no hesitation in asserting that the first federal enactment to experiment with a form of plea bargaining is the **Economic and Financial Crimes Commission (Establishment) Act (EFCC Act)**.[310]

The provision of **Section 14 (2) of the EFCC Act** indicates that when a defendant agrees to give up money stolen by him; the Commission may compound any offence for which such a person is charged under the Act. This provision has no universal application to all criminal trials in Nigeria as negotiations there under are expressly limited to offences punishable under the EFCC Act.

Sections 14-18 of the EFCC Act provides for crimes for which the Commission can exercise jurisdiction. These includes: offences relating to financial malpractices, offences in relation to terrorism, offences relating to public officers' retention of proceeds of criminal conduct and offences in relation to economic and financial crimes.

The statutory blessing given to plea bargaining in Nigeria is not limited to the EFCC Act. In fact, the most commendable step in giving statutory back up to plea bargain in Nigeria is the enactment of the **Administration of Criminal Justice Law 2011,**

---

[310] Economic and Financial Crimes Commission (Establishment) Act 2004, s. 1.

Laws of Lagos State, which institutionalized plea bargain in Lagos State. For the purpose of proper understanding and appreciation of the position in Lagos, this paper would reproduce the relevant sections of the aforementioned law:

76(1) The prosecutor and a defendant or his legal practitioner may before the plea to the charge, enter into an agreement in respect of:

(a) a plea of guilty by the defendant to the offence charged or a lesser offence of which he may be convicted on the charge, and

(b) an appropriate sentence to be imposed by the Court if the defendant is convicted of the offence to which he intends to plead guilty.

(2) The prosecutor may only enter into an agreement contemplated in subsection (1) of this Section: (a) after consultation with the Police Officer responsible for the investigation of the case and if reasonably feasible, the victim, and

(b) with due regard to the nature of and circumstances relating to the offence, the defendant and the interest of the community.

(3) The prosecutor, if reasonably feasible shall afford the complainant or his representative the opportunity to make representations to the prosecutor regarding

(a) the contents of the agreement; and

(b) the inclusion in the agreement of a compensation or restitution order.

(4) An agreement between the parties contemplated in subsection (1) shall be reduced to writing and shall:

(a) state that, before conclusion of the agreement, the defendant has been informed (i) that he has a right to remain silent; (ii) of the consequences of not remaining silent; (iii) that he is not obliged to make any confession or admission that could be used in evidence against him.

(b) state fully the terms of the agreement and any admissions made and,

(c) be signed by the prosecutor, the defendant, the legal practitioner and the interpreter as the case may be.

(5) The Presiding Judge, or Magistrate before whom criminal proceedings are pending shall not participate in the discussions contemplated in subsection (1). Provided that he may be approached by Counsel regarding the contents of the discussions and he may inform them in general terms of the possible advantages of discussions, possible sentencing options or the acceptability of a proposed agreement.

(6) Where a plea agreement is reached by the prosecution and defence, the prosecutor shall inform the court that the parties have reached an agreement and the Presiding Judge or Magistrate shall then inquire from the defendant to confirm the correctness of the agreement.

(7) The Presiding Judge or Magistrate shall ascertain whether the defendant admits the allegations in the charge to which he has pleaded guilty and whether he entered into the agreement voluntarily and without undue influence and may:

(a) if satisfied that the defendant is guilty of the offence to which he has pleaded guilty, convict the defendant on his plea of guilty to that offence, or;

(b) if he is for any reason of the opinion that the defendant cannot be convicted of the offence in respect of which the agreement was reached and to which the defendant has pleaded guilty or that the agreement is in conflict with the defendant's rights referred to in subsection (4) of this Section, he shall record a plea of not guilty in respect of such charge and order that the trial proceed.

(8) Where a defendant has been convicted in terms of subsection (7) (a), the Presiding Judge or Magistrate shall consider the sentence agreed upon in the agreement and if he is:

(a) satisfied that such sentence is an appropriate sentence impose the sentence, or:

(b) of the view that he would have imposed a lesser sentence than the sentence agreed upon in the agreement impose the lesser sentence; or

(c) of the view that the offence requires a heavier sentence than the sentence agreed upon in the agreement, he shall inform the defendant of such heavier sentence he considers to be appropriate.

(9) Where the defendant has been informed of the heavier sentence as contemplated in subsection (8) above, the defendant may:

(a) abide by his plea of guilty as agreed upon in the agreement and agree that, subject to the defendant's right to lead evidence and to present argument relevant to sentencing, the Presiding Judge, or Magistrate proceed with the sentencing; or

(b) withdraw from his plea agreement, in which event the trial shall proceed de novo before another Presiding Judge, or Magistrate, as the case maybe.

(10) Where a trial proceeds as contemplated under subsection (9) (a) or de novo before another Presiding Judge, or Magistrate as contemplated in subsection (9) (b):

(a) no reference shall be made to the agreement;

(b) no admissions contained therein or statements relating thereto shall be admissible against the defendant; and

(c) the prosecutor and the defendant may not enter into a similar plea and sentence agreement.

Plea bargaining has secured convictions in high-profile cases, including Federal Republic of Nigeria v. Cecilia Ibru, Federal Republic of Nigeria v. Alamieyeseigha, Federal Republic of Nigeria v. Tafa Balogun and Federal Republic of Nigeria v. Lucky Igbinedion.

In the case of Federal Republic of Nigeria v. Cecilia Ibru, the commission had charged Mrs Cecilia Ibru with a twenty-five-count criminal information offence bordering on financial crimes before the court. However, she entered into a plea bargain with the prosecution and pleaded guilty to a lesser three-count charge. The court thereafter convicted Ibru on the three-count charge and ordered the forfeiture of her assets, which amounted to about one hundred and ninety-one billion naira. She was sentenced to six months in prison for each of the three counts, to be served concurrently. In effect, Ibru was expected to spend only six months in jail.[311]

Another plea bargain under the EFCC Act was the former governor of Bayelsa State, Alamieyeseigha, who stood trial on a thirty-three-count charge of corruption, money laundering, illegal acquisition of property and false declaration of assets. He pleaded guilty to a six-count charge of money laundering brought by the commission and forfeited properties worth billions of naira in exchange for the lesser sentence. The former governor entered into a plea bargain with the commission, gave up his right to a trial and pleaded guilty to the charges. Rather than serving a prolonged prison term if convicted, he accepted the commission's

---

[311] K. Oladele, *'Plea bargaining and the criminal justice system in Nigeria'* (http://www.vanguardngr.com October 14, 2010) http://www.vanguardngr.com/2010/10/plea-bargaining-and-the-criminal-justice-system-in-nigeria/, accessed July 4, 2014.

offer for a guilty plea. However, because he had completed almost two years in jail before accepting the bargain, he was released a few days after his conviction.[312]

Other beneficiaries of plea bargains in Nigeria include Tafa Balogun, the former inspector general of police and Mr Lucky Igbinedion, the former governor of Edo State.[313]

As shown in the cases cited, plea bargaining has proven useful in Nigeria's criminal justice system by saving time and avoiding the necessity of public trials, thereby protecting innocent victims of crime from the ordeal of giving evidence during trials. The use of plea bargaining in these cases has yielded fruits, one of which was the reduction of public expenditure that would have been incurred during prolonged trials.

If the cases had gone to full trial, there would have been an unacceptable waste of state resources as trials are so costly. Lawyers are paid appearance fees each time they appear in court for a case. The commission usually hires the services of senior advocates of Nigeria, so one can imagine how much money would have been spent if these cases had gone to full trial. So, we can appreciate Tafa Balogun and the rest who chose to accept the plea bargains.

This has also helped decongest prisons. Overcrowding in Nigeria's prisons is no longer news. The prisons have poor sanitary systems, and they rarely have facilities; where facilities do exist, they are dilapidated and unhygienic.

Despite the advantages noted above, the concept of plea bargaining has been criticized by a number of people. The most notable among them is the former chief justice of Nigeria (CJN),

---

312 Ibid.
313 Ibid.

Justice Dahiru Musdapher, who was reported to have criticized the commission for smuggling the plea bargain concept into Nigerian criminal jurisprudence and also said that the concept had 'dubious' origins. The former CJN explained that he meant that the concept had a dubious origin in Nigeria.

> *When I described the concept of 'dubious origin', I was not referring to the original raison d'être or the juridical motive behind its conception way back, either in the United States or in England in the early nineteenth century; I was referring to the sneaky motive behind its introduction into our legal system, or its evident fraudulent application. You will learn that plea bargain is not only 'condemnation without adjudication', as John Langbien decried it; it is, as some other critics say, 'a triumph of administrative and organizational interests over justice'. At its very best, it penalizes the innocent who may be tempted to plead guilty to avoid being actuated by judicial default, and, at its most obnoxious extent, it grants 'undue leniency' as reward to criminals simply for pleading their guilt. You will see also that plea bargain is not only a flagrant subordination of the public's interest to the interest of 'criminal justice administration', but, worst of all, the concept generally promotes a cynical view of the entire legal system. I have said that our wavering disposition on the ethical standards set by your noble profession guarantees or jeopardizes our peace, security and progress. And it is the reason that I have chosen this occasion to speak—with all sense of solemnity—on a matter that has continued to eat away at even the modest gains that we seem to be making in reforming*

> *both the infrastructure and the overall judicial template of the Nigerian Judiciary.*[314]

The commission did not smuggle the concept into Nigeria. The lawmakers carved laws around the concept of plea bargaining, and the commission capitalized on those provisions to the country's advantage by applying them to the cases they were dealing with for the benefit of Nigeria and Nigerians.

The concept of plea bargaining did not have a 'dubious' origin in the sense that there was not a sneaky motive behind its introduction into Nigeria's legal system, nor was its application fraudulent. This is a new age in which alternative dispute resolutions are taking the place of litigation. Plea bargaining is like the alternative dispute resolution that is used in a civil trial. It saves the court time and money.

Plea bargaining does, however, penalize the innocent who may be tempted to plead guilty. Prosecutors could try to intimidate defendants by drawing up countless numbers of charges, thus forcing innocent defendants to submit to the plea bargain offers, which is complete injustice. This can be avoided if the defendants become more enlightened about the bag of tricks the prosecutors could attempt to play on them.

8.4.2 UNITED STATES

The **Federal Rules of Criminal Procedure 2010,** and in specific, **Rule 11 (c),** recognizes and codifies the concept of plea agreements in the United States.

One recent estimate indicated that guilty pleas account for the disposition of as many as 95% of all criminal cases in United

---

[314]D. A. Akintimoye, *'Should plea bargaining be abolished or encouraged in Nigeria?'* (http://community.vanguardngr.com March 7, 2012) http://community.vanguardngr.com/profiles/blogs/should-plea-bargaining-be-abolished-or-encouraged-in-nigeria, accessed January 2, 2014.

States. A substantial number of these are the result of plea discussions.[315]

While some scholars have interpreted the above statistics to mean that the process of plea bargaining is been abused in the American Criminal Justice System.[316] The statistics could be interpreted to mean that the concept of plea bargaining has been properly administered in the United States.

The basis for such interpretation lies in **subdivision (c) Rule 11** of the **U.S. Federal Rules of Criminal Procedure 2010.**

The procedure described in subdivision (c) is designed to prevent abuse of plea discussions and agreements by providing appropriate and adequate safeguards.

Subdivision (c) (1) specifies that the "attorney for the government and the attorney for the defendant or the defendant when acting pro se may" participate in plea discussions. The inclusion of "the defendant when acting pro se" is intended to reflect the fact that there are situations in which a defendant insists upon representing himself. It may be desirable that an attorney for the government not enter plea discussions with a defendant personally. If necessary, counsel can be appointed for purposes of plea discussions. **Subdivision (b) (2)** makes it mandatory that the court inquire of the defendant whether his plea is the result of plea discussions between him and the attorney for the government. This is intended to enable the court to reject an agreement reached by an unrepresented defendant unless the court is satisfied that acceptance of the agreement adequately protects the rights of the defendant and the interests of justice.

---

315 G Fields and J R. Emshwiller, *'Federal Guilty Pleas, Soar As Bargains Trump Trials'* (http://online.wsj.com 23rd September 2012) http://online.wsj.com/news/articles/SB10000872396390443589304577637610097206808 Accessed 7th October 2014.

316 T Lynch, '*The Case against Plea Bargaining*' (Regulation Fall 2003) 24

Apparently, it is the practice of most prosecuting attorneys to enter plea discussions only with defendant's counsel. Discussions without benefit of counsel increase the likelihood that such discussions may be unfair. Some courts have indicated that plea discussions in the absence of defendant's attorney may be constitutionally prohibited.[317]

Subdivision (c) (2) provides that the judge shall require the disclosure of any plea agreement in open court.

Upon notice of the plea agreement, the court is given the option to accept or reject the agreement or defer its decision until receipt of the presentence report.

The judge may, and often should, defer his decision until he examines the presentence report. This is made possible by rule 32 which allows a judge, with the defendant's consent, to inspect a presentence report to determine whether a plea agreement should be accepted.

The plea agreement procedure does not attempt to define the criteria for the acceptance or rejection of a plea agreement. Such a decision is left to the discretion of the individual trial judge.

Subdivision (c)(4) makes is mandatory, if the court decides to accept the plea agreement, that it inform the defendant that it will embody in the judgment and sentence the disposition provided in the plea agreement, or one more favourable to the defendant. This serves the purpose of informing the defendant immediately that the agreement will be implemented.

Subdivision (c)(5) requires the court, if it rejects the plea agreement, to inform the defendant of this fact and to advise the defendant personally, in open court, that the court is not bound

---

[317] See Anderson v. North Carolina, 221 F.Supp. 930, 935 (W.D.N.C.1963); Shape v. Sigler, 230 F.Supp. 601, 606 (D.Neb. 1964).

by the plea agreement. The defendant must be afforded an opportunity to withdraw his plea and must be advised that if he persists in his guilty plea or plea of nolo contendere, the disposition of the case may be less favourable to him than that contemplated by the plea agreement.

If the court rejects the plea agreement and affords the defendant the opportunity to withdraw the plea, the court is not precluded from accepting a guilty plea from the same defendant at a later time, when such plea conforms to the requirements of rule 11.

In addition to Rule 11 (c) of the Federal Rules of Criminal Procedure, there are a number of cases decided by the U.S. Supreme Court on 21st March 2012, which support the above interpretation.

In the first case, **Missouri v. Frye,** defendant Galin Frye was charged with felony driving without a licence after several repeated offences. The State offered to reduce the charge to a misdemeanour with maximum jail time of one year in exchange for a guilty plea. Although prosecutors communicated this offer to Mr. Frye's attorney, the attorney made no effort to relay the offer to his client. As a result, the offer expired without Mr. Frye ever knowing of its existence. Mr. Frye later pled guilty without any agreement with the State, and he was sentenced to three years in prison.

The Supreme Court held that Mr. Frye was entitled to the effective assistance of counsel during plea negotiations and that **Strickland v. Washington** provides the appropriate standard for evaluating such a claim. Consequently, a prisoner pursuing such a claim must prove both deficient performance and prejudice. Citing to a number of sources, including the **ABA Criminal Justice Standards,** the Court found that an attorney's failure to communicate a plea offer to his client may constitute deficient performance. While evaluating deficient performance in Mr. Frye's case, the Court noted that there was no evidence that any effort was made to communicate the offer or that Mr. Frye interfered in any way with the communication of the offer.

Having found deficient performance, the Court then analysed whether Mr. Frye was prejudiced by his attorney's actions. In order to prove prejudice, the Court held that Mr. Frye must show a "reasonable probability" that 1) he would have accepted the offer had it been made known to him; 2) acceptance of the offer would have resulted in a less severe sentence; 3) the state would not have withdrawn or changed the offer; and 4) the trial court would have sentenced him according to the agreement. Although the Court found that Mr. Frye had likely satisfied the first two requirements, it expressed serious doubts that the State would not have withdrawn the offer or that the trial court would not have rejected it. Writing for the majority, Justice Kennedy pointed out a number of considerations, such as the fact that Mr. Frye was charged with another instance of the same offence while the case was pending and that Missouri law allows a trial judge to disregard a plea agreement during sentencing. Ultimately the Court found that the issue of prejudice in Mr. Frye's case turned on questions of state law and remanded the case for further proceedings.

A companion case, **Lafler v. Cooper,** was decided the same day as **Frye.** Anthony Cooper was charged by the state of Michigan with attempted murder for shooting a woman in her buttocks and leg. The prosecution offered a reduced sentence in exchange for a guilty plea, but Mr. Cooper's attorney advised him not to take it, erroneously instructing him that he could not be convicted of attempted murder because the victim was shot below the waist. Consequently, Mr. Cooper's case went to trial, where he was convicted and sentenced to a term 3.5 times longer than the sentence offered in the plea bargain. During state post-conviction proceedings, the court rejected the claim of ineffective assistance of counsel, its analysis turning on whether Mr. Cooper's rejection of the offer was voluntary. Mr. Cooper then filed a habeas petition with the federal district court, which applied the **Strickland** standard and found that he had been denied his Sixth Amendment right to counsel. The Sixth Circuit affirmed the district court's decision and ordered that Mr. Cooper be sentenced to the terms of the original plea offer.

The Supreme Court affirmed the Sixth Circuit's decision in part, holding that if a plea bargain is offered, a criminal defendant has a constitutional right to effective assistance of counsel in considering whether to accept that offer. It rejected the State's argument that a fair trial and sentencing by jury could correct the earlier constitutional error, noting that "the constitutional rights of criminal defendants . . . are granted to the innocent and the guilty alike." Again writing for the majority, Justice Kennedy limited his analysis to the question of prejudice and the appropriate remedy, because both parties conceded deficient performance.

Examining the same factors discussed in **Frye,** the Court agreed with the Sixth Circuit, finding Mr. Cooper had satisfied the prejudice prong of **Strickland**. The Court found that the Sixth Circuit erred, however, in determining the appropriate remedy. It held that, in this instance, the State should re-offer the plea bargain, and if accepted by the defendant, the trial court could then exercise its discretion in issuing a sentence. Justice Kennedy suggested that this discretion is very broad, indicating that the court may issue a sentence ranging anywhere from the terms of the plea agreement to the original sentence being challenged by the defendant. He declined to discuss the "boundaries of proper discretion," finding that this would be best informed by state law.

The Court vacated the Sixth Circuit's judgment and remanded for further proceedings.

Both cases were decided by a 5-4 majority of the court, with Justice Scalia writing dissents in each case joined by Justices Thomas and Roberts, and Justice Alito dissenting separately in **Lafler.**[318]

8.4.3 UNITED KINGDOM

The concept of 'plea bargaining' traditionally has no legal standing in the law of England and Wales. However, informal 'discussions' between Counsel on both sides will often lead to an 'offer' by the defence to enter a plea of guilty to either a lesser count or to an agreed basis of plea.

Normally, the first occasion at which a defendant is required to enter a plea is at the Plea and Case Management Hearing in the Crown Court. The defendant may enter a guilty plea at the hearing, and may subsequently change his plea to guilty at any time before a trial commences or even during the trial process.

A plea of guilty must be entered voluntarily. If the accused is deprived of a genuine choice as to plea and in consequence purports to plead guilty, the plea is a nullity and the conviction can be quashed on appeal.[319]

The above procedure ensures that plea discussions are not being abused in the United Kingdom's Criminal Justice System.

Some recent developments have sought to formalise the process of plea bargaining in the United Kingdom. A 'Goodyear

---

[318] E M Williams, *'U.S. Supreme Court Recognizes Right to Effective Counsel in Plea Bargains'* (http://www.americanbar.org) http://www.americanbar.org/publications/project_press/2012/spring/plea_bargains.html Accessed 1st October 2014.

[319] The SFO Operational Handbook 2012.

application' enables the accused to seek, and the Judge, if he feels it appropriate, to provide an indication of sentence. The following guidelines are given in **R v. Goodyear [2005] 1 WLR 2532:**

i. A Court should not give an indication of sentence unless one has been sought by the accused.

ii. The Court remains entitled to exercise the power to indicate that the sentence, or type of sentence, on the accused would be the same whether the case proceeds as a plea of guilty or goes to trial with a resulting conviction. The Court is also entitled to remind the defence advocate that the accused is entitled to seek an advance indication of sentence.

iii. Where an indication is sought, the Court may refuse altogether to give an indication, or may postpone doing so, with or without giving reasons.

iv. Where the Court has it in mind to defer an indication, the probability is that the Judge would explain his reasons, and further indicate the circumstances in which, and when he would be prepared to respond to a request for a sentence indication.

v. If the Court refuses to give an indication it remains open to the defence to make a further request for an indication at a later stage. The Court should not normally initiate the process, except where appropriate to indicate that the circumstances have changed sufficiently to permit a renewed application for an indication.

vi. Once an indication has been given, it is binding.

vii. If the accused does not plead guilty, the indication will cease to have effect.

viii. Where appropriate, there must be an agreed, written basis of plea, otherwise the Judge should refuse to give an indication.[320]

The process laid down in R v. Goodyear [2005] 1 WLR 2532 is somewhat similar to plea bargaining, but it is not plea bargaining.

There is no actual agreement between the judge and the defendants to reduce the sentence if the defendants plead guilty. Also, there is no actual agreement between the prosecutors and the defendants to reduce the number of charges if the defendants plead guilty.

The only agreement is for the judge to reveal the details of judgment before the prescribed time.

8.5 CONCLUSION

The concept of plea bargaining has not been abused in Nigeria, the United States or the United Kingdom. Rather, it has been utilized in a coordinated way and, in the process, has made a positive impact on the criminal justice system of these countries. Plea bargaining has saved time and state resources, and although it has its disadvantages, the advantages completely outweigh them.

The United States has secured the highest number of convictions compared to Nigeria and the United Kingdom.

Therefore, Nigeria and the United Kingdom are recommended to adopt the US approach.

---

[320] The SFO Operational Handbook 2012.

CHAPTER 9

CUSTOMER DUE DILIGENCE

'Customer due diligence/know your customer' is intended to enable a financial institution to form a reasonable belief that it knows the true identity of each of its customers and, with an appropriate degree of confidence, knows the types of business and transactions the customer is likely to undertake.

The financial institution should have procedures in place to: (i) identify and verify the identity of each customer on a timely basis, (ii) take reasonable risk-based measures to identify and verify the identity of any beneficial owner and (iii) obtain appropriate additional information to understand the customer's circumstances and business, including the expected nature and level of transactions.[321]

Financial institutions are required to undertake customer due-diligence (CDD) measures when: (i) establishing business relations, (ii) carrying out occasional transactions above the applicable designated threshold (fifteen thousand US dollars or Euros) or that are wire transfers, (iii) there is a suspicion of money laundering or terrorist financing or (iv) the financial institution has doubts about the veracity of adequacy of previously obtained customer identification data.

The principle that financial institutions should conduct CDD should be set out in law. Each country may determine how it

[321] FATF Guidance on the Risk Based Approach to Combating Money Laundering and Terrorist Financing, (High Level Principles and Procedures) (2007), paragraph 3.10.

imposes specific CDD obligations, either through law or enforceable means.[322]

This chapter compares the approaches adopted in Nigeria, the United Kingdom and the United States as they relate to the application of CDD measures to determine what the best approach is.

The comparison falls under the following subheadings: 'Customer Information Required', 'Verification through Documents' and 'Verification through Nondocumentary Methods'.

9.1 CUSTOMER INFORMATION REQUIRED

9.1.1 NIGERIA

Financial institutions are required to obtain the following information in relation to natural persons:

i. Legal name and any other names used (such as maiden name);

ii. Permanent address (full address shall be obtained and the use of a post office box number only, is not sufficient);

iii. Telephone number, fax number and email address;

iv. Date and place of birth;

v. Nationality;

vi. Occupation, public position held and name of employer;

[322] The Financial Action Task Force (FATF): International Standards on Combating Money Laundering and the Financing of Terrorism and Proliferation, (The FATF Recommendations) 2012, Interpretive Note to Recommendation 10

vii. An official personal identification number or other unique identifier contained in an unexpired official document such as passport, identification card, residence permit, social security records or drivers' licence that bears a photograph of the customer;

viii. Type of account and nature of the banking relationship; and

ix. Signature.[323]

A financial institution shall make an initial assessment of a customer's risk profile from the information provided and particular attention shall be focused on those customers identified as having a higher risk profile and any additional inquiries made or information obtained in respect of those customers shall include:

i. Evidence of an individual's permanent address sought through a credit reference agency search, or through independent verification by home visits;

ii. Personal reference by an existing customer of the same institution;

iii. Prior bank reference and contact with the bank regarding the customer;

iv. Source of wealth; and

v. Verification of employment and public position held where appropriate.[324]

---

[323] CBN (Anti-Money Laundering and Combating the Financing of Terrorism in Banks and Other Financial Institutions in Nigeria) Regulations, 2013, Schedule II Paragraph 1 (1)

[324] CBN (Anti-Money Laundering and Combating the Financing of Terrorism in Banks and Other Financial Institutions in Nigeria) Regulations, 2013, Schedule II Paragraph 1 (5)

9.1.2 UNITED STATES

Financial institutions are required to obtain the following information in relation to natural persons:

i. Name;

ii. Date of birth;

iii. Address;

iv. Identification number.[325]

Customers that pose higher money laundering or terrorist financing risks present increased exposure to banks; due diligence policies, procedures, and processes should be enhanced as a result. Enhanced due diligence (EDD) for higher-risk customers is especially critical in understanding their anticipated transactions and implementing a suspicious activity monitoring system that reduces the bank's reputation, compliance, and transaction risks. Higher-risk customers and their transactions should be reviewed more closely at account opening and more frequently throughout the term of their relationship with the bank.

The bank may determine that a customer poses a higher risk because of the customer's business activity, ownership structure, anticipated or actual volume and types of[326] transactions, including those transactions involving higher-risk jurisdictions. If so, the bank should consider obtaining, both at account opening and throughout the relationship, the following information on the customer:

i. Purpose of the account;

ii. Source of funds and wealth;

---

325 Federal Financial Institutions Examination Council: Bank Secrecy Act/Anti-Money Laundering Examination Manual 2010, 54.

326 Federal Financial Institutions Examination Council: Bank Secrecy Act/Anti-Money Laundering Examination Manual 2010, 64.

iii. Individuals with ownership or control over the account, such as beneficial owners, signatories or guarantors;

iv. Occupation or type of business (of customer or other individuals with ownership or control over the account);

v. Financial statements;

vi. Banking references;

vii. Domicile (where the business is organized);

viii. Proximity of the customer's residence, place of employment, or place of business to the bank;

ix. Description of the customer's primary trade area and whether international transactions are expected to be routine;

x. Description of the business operations, the anticipated volume of currency and total sales, and a list of major customers and suppliers;

xi. Explanations for changes in account activity.[327]

9.1.3 UNITED KINGDOM

Firms are required to obtain the following information in relation to natural persons:

i. Full name;

ii. Residential address;

iii. Date of birth.[328]

---

327 Federal Financial Institutions Examination Council: Bank Secrecy Act/Anti-Money Laundering Examination Manual 2010, 65.

When someone becomes a new customer, or applies for a new product or service, or where there are indications that the risk associated with an existing business relationship might have increased, the firm should, depending on the nature of the product or service for which they are applying, request information as to:

i. The customers residential status;

ii. Employment and salary details;

iii. Other sources of income or wealth (e.g., inheritance, divorce settlement, property sale).[329]

9.2 VERIFICATION THROUGH DOCUMENTS

9.2.1 NIGERIA

Financial institutions shall verify the information referred to in subsection 9.1.1 by at least one of the following methods:

i. Confirming the date of birth from an official document (such as birth certificate, passport, identity card, social security records);

ii. Confirming the permanent address (such as utility bill, tax assessment, bank statement, a letter from a public authority).[330]

[328] The Joint Money Laundering Steering Group JMLSG, *Prevention of money laundering/ combating terrorist financing 2013* Revised Version, Guidance for the UK financial sector Part I, Amended November 2013, Paragraph 5.3.70

[329] The Joint Money Laundering Steering Group JMLSG, *Prevention of money laundering/ combating terrorist financing 2013* Revised Version, Guidance for the UK financial sector Part I, Amended November 2013, Paragraph 5.5.6

[330] CBN (Anti-Money Laundering and Combating the Financing of Terrorism in Banks and Other Financial Institutions in Nigeria) Regulations, 2013, Schedule II Paragraph 1 (2) (a) (b)

9.2.2 UNITED STATES

A bank using documentary methods to verify a customer's identity must have procedures that set forth the minimum acceptable documentation.

Banks shall verify the information referred to in subsection 9.1.2 by at least one of the following methods:

i. A Driver's licence;

ii. Passport.[331]

9.2.3 UNITED KINGDOM

If identity is to be verified from documents, this should be based on: Either a government-issued document which incorporates:

i. The customer's full name and photograph, and;

ii. Either his residential address;

iii. Or his date of birth

Or a government-issued document (without a photograph) which incorporates the customer's full name, supported by a second document, either government-issued, or issued by a judicial authority, a public sector body or authority, a regulated utility company, or another FCA-regulated firm in the UK financial services sector, or in an equivalent jurisdiction, which incorporates:

i. The customer's full name and;

ii. Either his residential address;

iii. Or his date of birth.

---

[331] Federal Financial Institutions Examination Council: *Bank Secrecy Act/Anti-Money Laundering Examination Manual* 2010, 55.

Government-issued documents with a photograph include:

i. Valid passport;

ii. Valid photo card driving licence (full or provisional);

iii. National identity card;

iv. Firearms certificate or shotgun licence;

v. Identity card issued by the Electoral Office for Northern Ireland.

Government-issued documents without a photograph include:

i. Valid (old style) full UK driving licence;

ii. Recent evidence of entitlement to a state or local authority-funded benefit (including housing benefit and council tax benefit), tax credit, pension, educational or other grants.

Other documents include

i. Instrument of a Court appointment (such as liquidator, or grant of probate);

ii. Current council tax demand letter, or statement;

iii. Current bank statements, or credit/debit card statements, issued by a regulated financial sector firm in the United Kingdom, EU or an equivalent jurisdiction (but not ones printed off the internet);

iv. Utility bills (but not ones printed off the internet).[332]

---

[332] The Joint Money Laundering Steering Group JMLSG, *Prevention of money laundering/ combating terrorist financing 2013* Revised Version, Guidance for the UK financial sector Part I, Amended November 2013, Paragraph 5.3.74

9.3 VERIFICATION THROUGH NON-DOCUMENTARY METHODS

9.3.1 NIGERIA

Financial institutions may verify the information referred to in subsection 9.1.1 by at least one of the following methods:

i. Contacting the customer by telephone, by letter or by email to confirm the information supplied after an account has been opened (such as a disconnected phone, returned mail, or incorrect e-mail address shall warrant further investigation);

ii. Confirming the validity of the official documentation provided through certification by an authorized person such as embassy official, notary public.[333]

9.3.2 UNITED STATES

Banks are not required to use non-documentary methods to verify a customer's identity. However, a bank using non-documentary methods to verify a customer's identity must have procedures that set forth the methods the bank will use.

Non-documentary methods may include:

i. Contacting a customer;

ii. Independently verifying the customer's identity through the comparison of information provided by the customer with information obtained from a customer reporting agency, public data base, or other source;

[333] CBN (Anti-Money Laundering and Combating the Financing of Terrorism in Banks and Other Financial Institutions in Nigeria) Regulations, 2013, Schedule II Paragraph 1 (2) (c) (d)

iii. Checking references with other financial institutions; and

iv. Obtaining a financial statement.[334]

9.3.3 UNITED KINGDOM

If identity is verified electronically, this should be by the firm, using as its basis the customer's full name, address and date of birth, carrying out electronic checks either direct, or through a supplier.[335]

A number of commercial agencies which access many data sources are accessible online by firms, and may provide firms with a composite and comprehensive level of electronic verification through a single interface. Such agencies use databases of both positive and negative information, and many also access high-risk alerts that utilise specific data sources to identify high-risk conditions, for example, known identity frauds or inclusion on a sanctions list. Some of these sources are, however, only available to closed user groups.[336]

Positive information (relating to full name, current address, date of birth) can prove that an individual exists, but some can offer a higher degree of confidence than others. Such information should include data from more robust sources - where an individual has to prove their identity, or address, in some way in order to be

---

[334] Federal Financial Institutions Examination Council: *Bank Secrecy Act/ Anti-Money Laundering Examination Manual* 2010, 55.

[335] The Joint Money Laundering Steering Group JMLSG, *Prevention of money laundering/ combating terrorist financing* 2013 Revised Version, Guidance for the UK financial sector Part I, Amended November 2013, Paragraph 5.3.79

[336] The Joint Money Laundering Steering Group JMLSG, *Prevention of money laundering/ combating terrorist financing* 2013 Revised Version, Guidance for the UK financial sector Part I, Amended November 2013, Paragraph 5.3.35

included, as opposed to others, where no such proof is required.[337]

Negative information includes lists of individuals known to have committed fraud, including identity fraud, and registers of deceased persons. Checking against such information may be necessary to mitigate against impersonation fraud.[338]

For an electronic check to provide satisfactory evidence of identity on its own, it must use data from multiple sources, and across time, or incorporate qualitative checks that assess the strength of the information supplied. An electronic check that accesses data from a single source (e.g., a single check against the Electoral Roll) is not normally enough on its own to verify identity.[339]

Before using a commercial agency for electronic verification, firms should be satisfied that information supplied by the data provider is considered to be sufficiently extensive, reliable and accurate. This judgement may be assisted by considering whether the provider meets all the following criteria:

i. it is recognised, through registration with the Information Commissioner's Office, to store personal data;
ii. it uses a range of positive information sources that can be called upon to link an applicant to both current and previous circumstances;

[337] The Joint Money Laundering Steering Group JMLSG, *Prevention of money laundering/ combating terrorist financing* 2013 Revised Version, Guidance for the UK financial sector Part I, Amended November 2013, Paragraph 5.3.36

[338] The Joint Money Laundering Steering Group JMLSG, *Prevention of money laundering/ combating terrorist financing* 2013 Revised Version, Guidance for the UK financial sector Part I, Amended November 2013, Paragraph 5.3.37

[339] The Joint Money Laundering Steering Group JMLSG, *Prevention of money laundering/ combating terrorist financing* 2013 Revised Version, Guidance for the UK financial sector Part I, Amended November 2013, Paragraph 5.3.38

iii. it accesses negative information sources, such as databases relating to identity fraud and deceased persons;

iv. it accesses a wide range of alert data sources; and

v. it has transparent processes that enable the firm to know what checks were carried out, what the results of these checks were, and what they mean in terms of how much certainty they give as to the identity of the subject.[340]

In addition, a commercial agency should have processes that allow the enquirer to capture and store the information they used to verify an identity.[341]

9.4 DISCUSSION

The previous sections compared the approaches adopted in Nigeria, the United Kingdom and the United States as they relate to the application of CDD measures.

This section will determine issues that arise from such a comparison.

9.4.1 MEANING OF 'CUSTOMER'

As stated above, financial institutions are required to apply the necessary CDD measures to their customers.

The term 'customer' is not expressly defined in the Nigerian or UK Money Laundering Regulations as it is defined in the US Bank Secrecy Act/Anti–Money Laundering Examination Manual 2010. Its meaning must be inferred from the definitions of

[340] The Joint Money Laundering Steering Group JMLSG, *Prevention of money laundering/ combating terrorist financing* 2013 Revised Version, Guidance for the UK financial sector Part I, Amended November 2013, Paragraph 5.3.39

[341] The Joint Money Laundering Steering Group JMLSG, *Prevention of money laundering/ combating terrorist financing* 2013 Revised Version, Guidance for the UK financial sector Part I, Amended November 2013, Paragraph 5.3.40

'business relationship' and 'occasional transaction', the context in which it is used in the United Kingdom and Nigerian Money Laundering Regulations and its everyday dictionary meaning.[342]

In general, the customer is the party, or parties, with whom the business relationship is established, or for whom the transaction is carried out. Where, however, there are several parties to a transaction, not all will necessarily be customers.[343]

A 'business relationship' is defined as a business, professional or commercial relationship between a firm and a customer that, when contact is established, the firm expects to have an element of duration. A relationship need not involve the firm in an actual transaction; giving advice may often constitute establishing a business relationship.[344]

An 'occasional transaction' means a transaction carried out other than in the course of a business relationship (e.g., a single foreign-currency transaction or an isolated instruction to purchase shares), amounting to fifteen thousand Euros or more, whether the transaction is carried out in a single operation or in several operations that appear to be linked.[345]

---

342 The Joint Money Laundering Steering Group JMLSG, *Prevention of money laundering/ combating terrorist financing* 2013 Revised Version, Guidance for the UK financial sector Part I, Amended November 2013, Paragraph 5.3.3

343 The Joint Money Laundering Steering Group JMLSG, *Prevention of money laundering/ combating terrorist financing* 2013 Revised Version, Guidance for the UK financial sector Part I, Amended November 2013, Paragraph 5.3.4

344 For United Kingdom laws, see Money Laundering Regulations 2007, Regulation 2 (1). See also the Joint Money Laundering Steering Group JMLSG, *Prevention of money laundering/ combating terrorist financing* 2013 Revised Version, Guidance for the UK financial sector Part I, Amended November 2013, Paragraph 5.3.5. For Nigerian laws, see Money Laundering Prohibition Act 2011 (as amended), s. 25. See also CBN (Anti–Money Laundering and Combating the Financing of Terrorism in Banks and Other Financial Institutions in Nigeria) Regulations, 2013, Regulation 132.

345 For United Kingdom laws, see Money Laundering Regulations 2007, Regulation 2 (1); See also the Joint Money Laundering Steering Group JMLSG, *Prevention of money laundering/ combating terrorist financing* 2013 Revised Version, Guidance for the UK

The United States, on the other hand, defines a customer as a person (an individual, a corporation, partnership, a trust, an estate or any other entity recognized as a legal person) who opens a new account; an individual who opens a new account for another individual who lacks legal capacity; or an individual who opens a new account for an entity that is not a legal person (e.g., a civic club). A customer does not include a person who does not receive banking services, such as a person whose loan application is denied. The definition of customer also does not include an existing customer as long as the bank has a reasonable belief that it knows the customer's true identity. Excluded from the definition of customer are federally regulated banks, banks regulated by a state bank regulator, governmental entities and publicly traded companies (as described in 31 CFR 103.22 (d) (2) (ii) through (iv).[346]

In view of the above facts, the US approach is far better than the United Kingdom and the Nigerian approach, because it leaves no room for ambiguity.

9.4.2 DIRECT DISCRIMINATION

This section aims to determine if the approaches adopted in Nigeria, the United States and the United Kingdom in relation to the application of CDD measures directly violate the human rights of customers.

We will look into the conditions that must be cumulatively met in order to be considered direct discrimination. These conditions include differential treatment, prohibited grounds, without

---

financial sector Part I, Amended November 2013, Paragraph 5.3.6. For Nigerian laws, see Money Laundering Prohibition Act 2011 (as amended), s. 25.

[346] Federal Financial Institutions Examination Council: *Bank Secrecy Act/Anti–Money Laundering Examination Manual* (2010), 53.

objective and reasonable justification and no reasonable relationship of proportionality.[347]

9.4.2.1 Differential Treatment

One of the conditions that must exist in direct discrimination is that there must be a given difference in treatment, which may concern the exercise of any right set forth by law.[348]

It could be argued that the UK law does create a difference in treatment by using the word *he* in paragraph 5.3.79 of its money laundering guidelines. That could imply that the CDD measures apply only to men, and not women.

However, since the law implements the FATF's Money Laundering Recommendations, which apply all anti–money laundering measures to both men and women, it does not discriminate.

The UK approach does not directly discriminate against customers, and, on that note, there is no need to further determine whether or not it meets the other direct discrimination requirements.

The US and Nigerian money laundering laws also do not directly discriminate against customers since both laws, unlike the UK law, never use the word *he*.

---

[347] Belgian Linguistic Case, (1979–80) 1 EHRR 252, Para 10; Swedish Engine Driver's Union v. Sweden (1979–80) 1 EHRR, 617, Para 45, 47, 48; National Union of Belgian Police v. Belgium (1979–80) 1 EHRR 578, Para 44, 46; Engel and Others v. The Netherlands (No.1) (1979–80) 1 EHRR 647, Para 72; The Republic of Ireland v. The United Kingdom (1979–80) 2 EHRR 25, Para 226.

[348] Belgian Linguistic Case (1979–80) 1 EHRR 252, Para 10; National Union of Belgian Police v. Belgium (1979–80) 1 EHRR 578 Para 44, 46.

9.5 CONCLUSION

In view of the arguments in the previous section, the following are recommended:

I. Nigeria and the United Kingdom should amend their money laundering laws by defining who a customer is.

II. The United Kingdom should amend its money laundering laws by removing the word *he*.

CHAPTER 10

RECORD KEEPING

The Financial Action Task Force (FATF) has advised countries to enact laws that mandate financial institutions to keep all records obtained through CDD measures (e.g., copies or records of official identification documents like passports, identity cards, driving licences or similar documents); account files and business correspondence, including the results of any analysis undertaken (e.g., inquiries to establish the background and purpose of complex, unusual large transactions) for at least five years after the business relationship ends or after the date of the occasional transaction.

Financial institutions should be required by law to maintain records on transactions and information obtained through the CDD measures. The CDD information and the transaction records should be available to domestic competent authorities upon appropriate authority.[349]

Although there is no material difference in the approaches adopted by Nigeria, the United States and the United Kingdom in relation to record-keeping requirements, it is still necessary to discuss this topic.

This chapter critically analyses the rule-based approach that is applied to record-keeping requirements under the subheading 'The Risk-Based Approach to Record-Keeping Requirements'.

---

349 The Financial Action Task Force (FATF): International Standards on Combating Money Laundering and the Financing of Terrorism and Proliferation, (The FATF Recommendations) 2012, Interpretive Note to Recommendation 11

10.1 THE RISK-BASED APPROACH TO RECORD-KEEPING REQUIREMENTS

The FATF requires financial institutions to apply a rule-based approach to record-keeping requirements. In other words, financial institutions are required by law to maintain records on transactions and information obtained through the CDD measures for a minimum period of five years.

A risk-based approach may be a preferable option to a rule-based approach.

A risk-based approach is designed to make it more difficult for money launderers and terrorist organizations to make use of financial institutions due to the increased focus on the identified higher-risk activities that are undertaken by these criminal elements.[350]

Countries should not be allowed to stipulate a minimum time frame for financial institutions to maintain records. Rather, the period should depend on whether or not the customer is high risk.

For customers who have been designated as higher risk by a firm, financial institutions should be allowed to keep records of information obtained through CDD measures for ten years or more. For customers designated as lower risk, financial institutions should be allowed to keep records of information obtained through CDD measures for as little as two years.

Keeping information for five years may lead to an unnecessary interference with a person's right to a private life, and such interference cannot be justified.

[350] FATF Guidance on the Risk Based Approach to Combating Money Laundering and Terrorist Financing, (High Level Principles and Procedures) (2007), paragraph 1.17.

10.2 CONCLUSION

In view of the arguments canvassed in section 10.1 of this chapter, a risk-based approach to record-keeping requirements is the preferable approach.

CHAPTER 11

LEVEL OF COMPLIANCE

The previous chapters focused on the anti–money laundering measures implemented by Nigeria, the United States and the United Kingdom for the purpose of combating money laundering and terrorist financing.

This chapter will determine the level of compliance with anti–money laundering measures in those countries.

11.1 NIGERIA

In a letter to banks and discount houses titled 'Status and Reporting Line of Chief Compliance Officers of Banks', with reference number: BSD/DIR/GEN/LAB/07/013, the Central Bank of Nigeria (CBN) stated that information available to it revealed that the qualifications of chief compliance officers of some banks and discount houses were below the grade of general manager that was required by the CBN.

Equally worrisome, the apex bank wrote, is that most of the compliance officers do not report directly to the board of directors, which is 'a flagrant disregard to the extant laws and regulations on the subject'.[351]

---

[351] C. Nweze, *'CBN laments skills gap of Compliance Officers'* (http://thenationonlineng.net May 29, 2014) http://thenationonlineng.net/new/cbn-laments-skills-gap-compliance-officers/, accessed October 1, 2014.

11.2 UNITED STATES

Examination authority over banks and other depository institutions for Bank Secrecy Act compliance has been delegated by[352] FinCEN to the industry's five functional regulators.

These regulators include the Board of Governors of the Federal Reserve System (Federal Reserve), the Federal Deposit Insurance Corporation, the National Credit Union Association, the Office of the Comptroller of the Currency and the Office of Thrift Supervision. State-chartered private banks, trust companies and credit unions without federal insurance have no federal functional regulators and come under the purview of the IRS SB/SE Division for purposes of BSA examination.

In the second half of 2004, US federal banking regulators completed forty-four public enforcement actions involving Bank Secrecy Act (BSA) violations.

Among the problems most often cited was the lack of independent testing to validate BSA compliance. In about 60 percent of the BSA cases that were closed in the second half, a bank was ordered to arrange for testing or was cited for failure to do so. In recent years, several banks have faced severe criminal and civil penalties as a consequence of BSA lapses.[353]

11.3 UNITED KINGDOM

The Financial Conduct Authority's 2011 thematic review of the management of high money laundering risk situations found that three quarters of the banks reviewed, including a number of major banks, were not managing this risk effectively. Around a third of banks, including the private banking arms of some major

---

352 US Money Laundering Threat Assessment (2005), 4.
353 US Money Laundering Threat Assessment (2005), 5.

banking groups, appeared willing to accept high levels of money laundering risk if the immediate reputational and regulatory risk was acceptable.[354]

Over half the banks the Financial Conduct Authority (FCA) visited failed to apply meaningful enhanced due-diligence (EDD) measures in higher-risk situations and so failed to identify or record adverse information about the customer or the customer's beneficial owner. Around a third of them dismissed serious allegations about their customers without adequate review. More than a third of the banks visited failed to put effective measures in place to identify customers as PEPs.[355]

Three quarters of the banks in the FCA's sample failed to take adequate measures to establish the legitimacy of the source of wealth and source of funds to be used in the business relationship. This was of particular concern where the bank was aware of significant adverse information about the customer's or beneficial owner's integrity.[356]

More recently, the FCA's thematic review of the control of financial crime risks in trade finance found that most banks, including a number of major UK banks, were not giving adequate attention to money laundering red flags in trade finance transactions. There was an inconsistent approach to risk assessment and only a few banks had conducted a specific trade finance money laundering risk assessment.[357]

---

354 Financial Conduct Authority: Anti–Money Laundering annual report (2013), Paragraph 6.2.
355 Financial Conduct Authority: Anti–Money Laundering annual report (2013), Paragraph 6.3.
356 Financial Conduct Authority: Anti–Money Laundering annual report (2013), Paragraph 6.4.
357 Financial Conduct Authority: Anti–Money Laundering annual report (2013), Paragraph 6.6.

About half of the banks had no clear policies or procedures document for dealing with trade-based money laundering risks. As a result, some banks failed to implement adequate controls to identify potentially suspicious transactions. Many banks were unable to demonstrate that money laundering risk had been taken into account when processing particular transactions. In particular, trade processing staff in most banks made inadequate use of customer due-diligence information that the relationship managers or trade sales teams gathered. In addition, systems and controls over dual-use goods were inadequate at most banks. However, a minority of banks used some innovative and effective techniques to assess money laundering risk in trade finance transactions, which other banks could usefully follow.[358]

The root cause of these problems is often a failure in governance of money laundering risk, which leads, among other things, to inadequate anti–money laundering resources and a lack of (or poor quality) assurance work across the firm. This often focuses on whether processes have been followed rather than on the substance of whether good AML judgments are being made.[359]

The weakness the FCA sees in dealings with high-risk customers and PEPs is a serious and persistent problem in firms of all sizes. However, this issue manifests itself in different ways in different types of firms. Small firms often fail to collect enhanced due-diligence information, as required under the MLR 2007. Large firms, including those that have been subject to Systematic Anti–Money Laundering Programme (SAMLP) examinations, often collect adequate information but fail to assess it properly and/or make poor judgments about the money laundering risk this

[358] Financial Conduct Authority: Anti–Money Laundering annual report (2013), Paragraph 6.7.
[359] Financial Conduct Authority: Anti–Money Laundering annual report (2013), Paragraph 6.8.

information exposes, particularly where potential profits are high.[360]

The FCA also found weaknesses in firms of all sizes in establishing and corroborating the source of wealth or funds for high-risk customers. Too much reliance is often placed on the customers' explanations, even when they are subject to serious and credible allegations of criminal activity.[361]

11.4 DISCUSSION

The previous section summarized the findings from regulatory authorities on the degree of anti–money laundering compliance in Nigeria, the United States and the United Kingdom.

This section analyses the issues that arose from such findings, with the aim of determining if there is need for reform.

11.4.1 QUALIFICATION OF COMPLIANCE OFFICERS

The problem the United Kingdom seems to be facing with regard to compliance is that many banks refuse to apply meaningful enhanced due-diligence measures in higher-risk situations.

In the United States, the problem most often cited is the lack of independent testing to validate BSA compliance.

In Nigeria, the problem appears to be much bigger. The people who ought to be responsible for coordinating and monitoring day-to-day anti–money laundering compliance in financial institutions lack the required expertise to undertake the job.

360 Financial Conduct Authority: Anti–Money Laundering annual report (2013), Paragraph 6.9.

361 Financial Conduct Authority: Anti–Money Laundering annual report (2013), Paragraph 6.10.

The CBN has attempted to fix the problem by issuing a circular requiring all deposit money banks and discount houses to ensure:

I. That no chief compliance officer in the institution is below the grade of general manager without prior CBN approval;
II. That the chief compliance officer reports to the board of directors with dotted lines to the MD/CEO and without interlocking roles.

Accordingly, the particulars of all current chief compliance officers along with evidence of the CBN's approval and the reporting lines should be forwarded to the director of banking supervision within one week from the date of the circular, which was 23 May 2014.[362]

The CBN approach appears to be similar to that of the FCA's approach. In the United Kingdom, the role of a compliance officer has been designated by the FCA as a controlled function under section 59 of the Financial Services and Markets Act 2000 (FSMA). As a result, any person invited to perform that function must be individually approved by the FCA, on the application of the firm, before performing the function.[363]

11.5 CONCLUSION

In view of the arguments canvassed in section 11.4 of this chapter, the CBN should adopt the approach of the FCA by conducting annual thematic reviews of banking operations. This would keep them updated on the performance level of these institutions.

---

362 CBN: *Circular on Status and Reporting Line of Chief Compliance Officers of Banks* (2014).
363 Financial Conduct Authority Handbook, SYSC 6.3.10 G. See also The Joint Money Laundering Steering Group JMLSG, *Prevention of money laundering/ combating terrorist financing* 2013 Revised Version, Guidance for the UK financial sector Part I, Amended November 2013, Paragraph 3.7

APPENDIX 1

GLOSSARY OF TERMINOLOGY

Confiscation

The term *confiscation,* which includes forfeiture where applicable, means the permanent deprivation of funds or other assets by order of a competent authority or a court. Confiscation or forfeiture takes place through a judicial or administrative procedure that transfers the ownership of specified funds or other assets to be transferred to the State. In this case, the person(s) or entity(ies) that held an interest in the specified funds or other assets at the time of the confiscation or forfeiture loses all rights, in principle, to the confiscated or forfeited funds or other assets. Confiscation or forfeiture orders are usually linked to a criminal conviction or a court decision whereby the confiscated or forfeited property is determined to have been derived from or intended for use in a violation of the law.

Currency

Currency refers to banknotes and coins that are in circulation as a medium of exchange.

Designated nonfinancial businesses and professions

Designated non-financial businesses and professions means:

a) Casinos.

b) Real estate agents.

c) Dealers in precious metals.

d) Dealers in precious stones.

e) Lawyers, notaries, other independent legal professionals and accountants – this refers to sole practitioners, partners or employed professionals within professional firms. It is not meant to refer to 'internal' professionals that are employees of other types of businesses, nor to professionals working for government agencies, who may already be subject to AML/CFT measures.

f) Trust and Company Service Providers refers to all persons or businesses that are not covered elsewhere under these Recommendations, and which as a business, provide any of the following services to third parties:

- acting as a formation agent of legal persons;
- acting as (or arranging for another person to act as) a director or secretary of a company, a partner of a partnership, or a similar position in relation to other legal persons;
- providing a registered office; business address or accommodation, correspondence or administrative address for a company, a partnership or any other legal person or arrangement;
- acting as (or arranging for another person to act as) a trustee of an express trust or performing the equivalent function for another form of legal arrangement;
- acting as (or arranging for another person to act as) a nominee shareholder for another person.

Financial institutions

Financial institutions mean any natural or legal person who conducts as a business one or more of the following activities or operations for or on behalf of a customer:

1. Acceptance of deposits and other repayable funds from the public.
2. Lending.
3. Financial leasing.
4. Money or value transfer services.
5. Issuing and managing means of payment (e.g. credit and debit cards, cheques, traveller's cheques, money orders and bankers' drafts, electronic money).
6. Financial guarantees and commitments.
7. Trading in:
   (a) money market instruments (cheques, bills, certificates of deposit, derivatives etc.);
   (b) foreign exchange;
   (c) exchange, interest rate and index instruments;
   (d) transferable securities;
   (e) commodity futures trading.
8. Participation in securities issues and the provision of financial services related to such issues.
9. Individual and collective portfolio management.
10. Safekeeping and administration of cash or liquid securities on behalf of other persons.
11. Otherwise investing, administering or managing funds or money on behalf of other persons.

12. Underwriting and placement of life insurance and other investment related insurance.
13. Money and currency changing.

Money Service Business

Money Service Business includes currency dealers, money transmitters, cheque cashers, and issuers of travellers' cheques, money orders or stored value.

Smurfing

Smurfing is the act of breaking down a transaction into smaller transactions to avoid regulatory requirements or an investigation by the authorities.

Terrorist

The term *terrorist* refers to any natural person who: (i) commits, or attempts to commit, terrorist acts by any means, directly or indirectly, unlawfully and wilfully; (ii) participates as an accomplice in terrorist acts ; (iii) organises or directs others to commit terrorist acts ; or (iv) contributes to the commission of terrorist acts by a group of persons acting with a common purpose where the contribution is made intentionally and with the aim of furthering the terrorist act or with the knowledge of the intention of the group to commit a terrorist act.

Terrorist act

A *terrorist act* includes:

(a) an act which constitutes an offence within the scope of, and as defined in one of the following treaties: (i) Convention for the Suppression of Unlawful Seizure of

Aircraft (1970); (ii) Convention for the Suppression of Unlawful Acts against the Safety of Civil Aviation (1971); (iii) Convention on the Prevention and Punishment of Crimes against Internationally Protected Persons, including Diplomatic Agents (1973); (iv) International Convention against the Taking of Hostages (1979); (v) Convention on the Physical Protection of Nuclear Material (1980); (vi) Protocol for the Suppression of Unlawful Acts of Violence at Airports Serving International Civil Aviation, supplementary to the Convention for the Suppression of Unlawful Acts against the Safety of Civil Aviation (1988); (vii) Convention for the Suppression of Unlawful Acts against the Safety of Maritime Navigation (2005); (viii) Protocol for the Suppression of Unlawful Acts against the Safety of Fixed Platforms located on the Continental Shelf (2005); (ix) International Convention for the Suppression of Terrorist Bombings (1997); and (x) International Convention for the Suppression of the Financing of Terrorism (1999).

(b) any other act intended to cause death or serious bodily injury to a civilian, or to any other person not taking an active part in the hostilities in a situation of armed conflict, when the purpose of such act, by its nature or context, is to intimidate a population, or to compel a Government or an international organisation to do or to abstain from doing any act.

APPENDIX 2

BIBLIOGRAPHY

BOOKS

Akehurst M, A Modern Introduction to International Law (5th Edition, George Allen and Unwin (Publishers) Ltd 1984)

Alldridge P Money Laundering Law, Forfeiture, Confiscation, Civil Recovery, Criminal Laundering and Taxation of the proceeds of crime. (Hart Publishing 2003)

Ellinger E.P, MODERN BANKING LAW (5TH Edition, Oxford University Press 2011)

Elliott C and Quinn F, Contract Law (7th Edition Pearson Education Limited 2009)

Evans M D, International Law (3rd Edition Oxford University Press 2010)

Gardiner R K, International Law (First Published Pearson Education Ltd 2003)

Garner B.A, Black's Law Dictionary (8th Edition West, a Thomson business 2004)

Hopton D, MONEY LAUNDERING, A CONCISE GUIDE FOR ALL BUSINESS (2nd Edition, Ashgate Publishing Ltd 2007)

Horsey K and Rackley E, Tort Law (2nd Edition Oxford University Press 2011)

Jones, M A, Textbook on Torts (8th Edition Oxford University Press 2002)

Kalin W, Kunzli J 'The Law of International Human Rights Protection' (First Published, Oxford University Press 2009)

Kidner R, Casebook on Torts (12th Edition Oxford University Press 2012)

Lilley P, DIRTY DEALING THE UNTOLD TRUTH ABOUT GLOBAL MONEY LAUNDERING, INTERNATIONAL CRIME AND TERRORISM (3rd Edition, Kogan Page Limited, 2006)

Loughman B P, Sibery R A, Bribery and Corruption, Navigating the global risks (John Wiley and Sons 2012)

Mathers C, Crime School: Money Laundering, True Crime meets the world of Business and finance (Firefly Books U.S Inc 2004)

Nwadialo F, S.A.N, The Criminal Procedure of the Southern States of Nigeria (2nd Edition MIJ Professional Publishers Limited 1987)

Odibei F F, Cases and Materials on Human Rights Law (1st Edition Pearl Publishers 2011)

Rehman J 'International Human Rights Law' (2nd Edition Pearson Education Limited 2010)

Reid K, 'A Practitioners Guide to the European Convention on Human Rights' (3rd Edition Sweet and Maxwell Ltd 2008)

Rehman J, International Human Rights Law (2nd Edition Pearson Education Limited 2010)

Schutter O D, International Human Rights Law (First Published Cambridge University Press 2010)

Shaw M.N, International Law (5th Edition Cambridge University Press 2003)

Umozurike U.O, Introduction to International Law (3rd Edition, Spectrum Books Limited, 2005)

ARTICLES

Aigbovo O: Nigerian anti-corruption statutes: an impact assessment 2013 16 (1) JMLC 62 – 78.

Alschuler A, 'Plea Bargaining and its History' 1979, 79 Columbia Law Review

Alldridge P, The UK Bribery Act, 'The Caffeinated Younger Sibling of the FCPA' 2012, 73 (5) Ohio State Journal, 1181 - 1216

Aaronberg D, Higgins N, All hail the Bribery Act-the toothless wonder 2011,6, Arch Rev 5-6.

Breslin B: The Bribery Act 2010: raising the bar above the US Foreign Corrupt Practices Act 2010, 31 (11) Comp Law. 362 – 369

Butcher C: Bribery Act proves hot topic for legal advisers.2011.25(25) Lawyers 7

Choo KKR, 'Politically exposed persons (PEPs): risk and mitigation 2008, 11 (4) JMLC, 371 – 387'

De Wit J: A risked based approach to AML 2007 15 (2) JFR and C 156 – 165

Drinnan R Australia: Proposed reform to Australian Foreign Bribery Legislation 2012,2, IELR, 40 -42

Garner B A, Black's Law Dictionary (8th Edition West, a Thomson business 2004)

Geary J, PEPs – Lets get serious. 2010 13(2) JMLC 103 – 108

Greenberg TS: Stolen Asset Recovery, Politically Exposed Persons, A policy paper on strengthening preventive measures

Lordi J A, The Uk Bribery Act: Endless Jurisdictional Liability on Corporate Violators 2012 Vol 44 Case W Res J Int LL,955.

Lynch T, 'The Case against Plea Bargaining' (Regulation Fall 2003) 24

Marshall P, Part 7 of the Proceeds of Crime Act 2002: double criminality, Legal Certainty, Proportionality and trouble ahead. 2003 11 (2) JFC 111-126

Marshall P, 'Part 7 of the Proceeds of Crime Act 2002: double criminality, legal certainty, proportionality and trouble ahead' 2003, 11 (2) JFC 111, 115 - 116.

Marshall P, 'Criminal Conduct Under Part 7 of the Proceeds of Crime Act 2002: A Requirement For Double Criminality'? (2003) 6 JIBFL 233

Marchini R: The new UK Bribery Act and data protection issues involving associated persons including suppliers and employees. 2011, 11 (8), WDPR 9 – 11

Nweze C, 'CBN laments skills gap of Compliance Officers' (http://thenationonlineng.net 29th May 2014) http://thenationonlineng.net/new/cbn-laments-skills-gap-compliance-officers/ Accessed 1st of October 2014

Otusanya OJ: 'The Role of offshore financial centres in elite money laundering practices: evidence from Nigeria. 2012,15(3) JMLC, 336 – 361'

Wells C: Bribery: Corporate Liability under the draft bill 2009.2009 7, Crim LR 479 – 487

Williams E M, 'U.S. Supreme Court Recognizes Right to Effective Counsel in Plea Bargains' (http://www.americanbar.org) http://www.americanbar.org/publications/project_press/2012/spring/plea_bargains.html Accessed 1st October 2014

Yeoh P: Bribery Act 2010: Implications for regulated firms (Legislative Comment) 2012 20 (3), JFR and C, 264 – 277

ELECTRONIC SOURCES

Aon Plc (2013): http://www.aon.com/about-aon/about-aon.jsp Accessed on 20th May 2013

Akintimoye D A, 'Should plea bargaining be abolished or encouraged in Nigeria?' (http://community.vanguardngr.com 7th March 2012) http://community.vanguardngr.com/profiles/blogs/should-plea-bargaining-be-abolished-or-encouraged-in-nigeria Accessed 2nd January 2014

Basel Committee on Banking Supervision, 'About the Basel Committee' (http://www.bis.org 20th June 2014) http://www.bis.org/bcbs/about.htm Accessed 10th September 2014

Daily Lives and Corruption: Public Opinion in Southern Africa by Transparency International 2011: http://corruptionwatch.org.za/sites/default/files/ti_public_opinion_corruption_sa_111122.pdf Accessed 15th May 2013

Financial Action Task Force, 'About us' (http://www.fatf-gafi.org) http://www.fatf-gafi.org/pages/aboutus/ Accessed 10th September 2014

Growing Beyond: a place for integrity 12th Global Survey by Ernst and Young 2012: http://www.ey.com/Publication/vwLUAssets/Global-Fraud-Survey-a-place-for-integrity-12th-Global-Fraud-Survey/$FILE/EY-12th-GLOBAL-FRAUD-SURVEY.pdf Accessed 15th May 2013

Hebert Smith Asia's anti-corruption report issue 1 Summer 2012: https://www.icsaglobal.com/assets/files/AsiaanticorruptionreportIssue1.pdf Accessed 15th May 2013

HM Revenue and Customs, 'Going through customs' (http://www.hmrc.gov.uk) http://www.hmrc.gov.uk/customs/arriving/customs-channels.htm Accessed 7th September 2014

International Association of Insurance Supervisors, 'About the IAIS' (http://www.iaisweb.org) http://www.iaisweb.org/About-the-IAIS-28 Accessed 10th September 2014

International Monetary Fund, 'Anti-Money Laundering/Combating the Financing of Terrorism' (https://www.imf.org) https://www.imf.org/external/np/leg/amlcft/eng/ Accessed 28th September 2014

International Monetary Fund, 'About the IMF' (http://www.imf.org) http://www.imf.org/external/about/ourwork.htm Accessed 10th September 2014

International Monetary Fund, 'The IMF and the Fight Against Money Laundering and the Financing of Terrorism' (https://www.imf.org 5th September 2014) https://www.imf.org/external/np/exr/facts/aml.htm Accessed 28th September 2014

Joseph O, 'Why encourage plea bargaining?' (http://www.punchng.com, 2nd September 2012) http://www.punchng.com/opinion/letters/why-encourage-plea-bargaining/ Accessed 3rd July 2014

Montaldo C, 'The plea bargain stage of a criminal case, stages of the criminal justice system' (http://crime.about.com) http://crime.about.com/od/Crime_101/a/The-Plea-Bargain-Stage-Of-A-Criminal-Case.htm Accessed 4th July 2014

Nigeria Customs Service, 'Passenger's Concessions' (https://www.customs.gov.ng) https://www.customs.gov.ng/Stakeholders/passengers_concessions.php Accessed 7th September 2014

Oladele K, 'Plea bargaining and the criminal justice system in Nigeria' (http://www.vanguardngr.com 14th October 2010) http://www.vanguardngr.com/2010/10/plea-bargaining-and-the-criminal-justice-system-in-nigeria/ Accessed 4th July 2014

Olin D, 'The Way We Live Now: 9-29-02: Crash Course; Plea Bargain' (http://www.nytimes.com 29th September 2002) http://www.nytimes.com/2002/09/29/magazine/the-way-we-live-now-9-29-02-crash-course-plea-bargain.html Accessed 3rd July 2014

R L Cassin: Understanding the KBR Halliburton Charges (The FCPA Blog, 24th February 2009) http://fcpablog.squarespace.com/blog/2009/2/24/understanding-the-kbr-halliburton-charges.html Accessed 16th May 2013

Stewart P and Wroughton L 'How Boko Haram is beating U.S efforts to choke its financing' (http://www.reuters.com 1st July 2014) http://www.reuters.com/article/2014/07/01/us-usa-nigeria-bokoharam-insight-idUSKBN0F636920140701 Accessed 5th of August 2014

The Criminalisation of Bribery in Asia and the Pacific: Frameworks and Practices in 28 Asian and Pacific Jurisdictions. Thematic Review – Final Report by ADB/OECD Anti-Corruption initiative for Asia and the Pacific 2010: http://www.oecd.org/site/adboecdanti-corruptioninitiative/46485272.pdf Accessed 15th May 2013

The International Organization of Securities Commissions, 'General Information' (http://www.iosco.org) http://www.iosco.org/about/ Accessed 10th of September 2014

The World Bank, 'What we do' (http://www.worldbank.org) http://www.worldbank.org/en/about/what-we-do Accessed 10th September 2014

The World Bank, 'Comprehensive Reference Guide to AML/CFT' (http://web.worldbank.org) http://web.worldbank.org/WBSITE/EXTERNAL/TOPICS/EXTFINANCIALSECTOR/EXTAML/0,,contentMDK:20746893~menuPK:2495265~pagePK:210058~piPK:210062~theSitePK:396512,00.html Accessed 10th September 2014

The Law Commission (LAW Com No 313) Reforming Bribery 2008: ***lawcommission****.justice.gov.uk/docs/cp185_****Reforming_Bribery****_report.pdf Accessed 15th May 2013*

Transparency International, 'The Global Coalition against Corruption' (http://www.transparency.org/cpi2013) http://www.transparency.org/cpi2013/results Accessed 26th June 2014.

Transparency International, Óverview' (http://www.transparency.org) http://www.transparency.org/whoweare/organisation Accessed 10th September 2014

U.S Department of Homeland Security, 'Declaring currency when entering the U.S in-transit to a foreign destination' (https://help.cbp.gov) https://help.cbp.gov/app/answers/detail/a_id/778/~/declaring-currency-when-entering-the-u.s.-in-transit-to-a-foreign-destination Accessed 7th September 2014

Willis Limited (2013) http://www.willis.com/Regulation/ accessed 15th May 2013

Wolfsberg Group, 'Global Banks: Global Standards' (http://www.wolfsberg-principles.com/) http://www.wolfsberg-principles.com/ Accessed 28th September 2014

INDEX

C

Cash Couriers
Declaration system, 5.1
Differential treatment, 5.2.2.1
Green Exit, 5.1.1.1
Prohibited grounds, 5.2.2.2
Protecting the financial system against money launderers/terrorists, 5.2.1
Red Exit, 5.1.1.2
Upholding equality before the law, 5.2.2
When to use the blue channel, 5.1.3.1
When to use the green channel, 5.1.3.2
When to use the red channel or red-point phone, 5.1.3.3
Without objective and reasonable justification, 5.2.2.3

Compliance Officers
Duties and responsibilities, 6.2
The title of the individual responsible for anti-money laundering compliance, 6.1

Confiscation Measures
Definition of plea bargaining, 8.1
History of plea bargaining, 8.2
The nature of plea bargaining, 8.3

Customer Due Diligence
Customer information required, 9.1
Direct discrimination, 9.4.2
Differential treatment, 9.4.2.1
Meaning of 'customer', 9.4.1

Verification through documents, 9.2
Verification through non-documentary methods, 9.3

D

Direct Discrimination
Differential treatment, 4.2.2.1, 5.2.2.1, 9.4.2.1
No reasonable relationship of proportionality, 4.2.2.4
Prohibited grounds, 4.2.2.2, 5.2.2.2
Without objective and reasonable justification, 4.2.2.3, 5.2.2.3

E

Enhanced Due Diligence (EDD)
Source of funds, 1.4.3.2
Source of wealth, 1.4.3.2
Implications of failure of a firm to conduct EDD, 1.4.4

Enhanced On-going Monitoring (EOM)
Aim of monitoring, 1.4.3.4
Implications of failure of a firm to conduct EOM, 1.4.4

I

International Bodies/Organisations
Basel Committee, 1.5.2
Financial Action Task Force, 1.5.1
International Monetary Fund, 1.5.4
International Association of Insurance Supervisors, 1.5.7
The Wolfsberg Group of International Financial Institutions, 1.5.3
The World Bank, 1.5.5
The International Organization of Securities Commission, 1.5.6
Transparency International, 1.5.8

L

Level of Compliance
Qualification of compliance officers, 11.4.1

M

Money Laundering
Stages of money laundering, 1.2
What is money laundering?, 1.1

Money Laundering Offence
Predicate offences for money laundering (domestic crimes), 3.2
Predicate offences for money laundering (foreign crimes), 3.3
Penalties, 3.4
The crime of money laundering, 3.1

P

Plea Bargaining
Definition of plea bargaining, 8.1
History of plea bargaining, 8.2
The nature of plea bargaining, 8.3

Politically Exposed Persons
Application of the PEPs definition, 4.1
Differential treatment, 4.2.2.1
No reasonable relationship of proportionality, 4.2.2.4
Prohibited grounds, 4.2.2.2
Protecting the financial system against corrupt PEPs, 4.2.1
Without objective and reasonable justification, 4.2.2.3
Upholding equality before the law, 4.2.2

R

Record Keeping
The Risk Based Approach to record keeping requirements, 10.1

Relevant Money Laundering Laws/Regulations
Nigeria, 2.1.1
United States, 2.1.2
United Kingdom, 2.1.3

Reporting Requirements
Confidentiality of STRs/tipping off (general rule), 2.2.1.4, 2.2.2.4, 2.2.3.4
Confidentiality of STRs/tipping off (exception), 2.2.1.5, 2.2.2.5, 2.2.3.5
Penalty, 2.2.1.6, 2.2.2.6, 2.2.3.6
What to file, 2.2.1.1, 2.2.2.1, 2.2.3.1
Where to file, 2.2.1.2, 2.2.2.2, 2.2.3.2
When to file, 2.2.1.3, 2.2.2.3, 2.2.3.3
When a transaction requires reporting, 2.3.2

Risk Assessment
Analysis of specific risk categories, 1.4.2
Identification of specific risk categories, 1.4.1

S

Senior Management Approval
The FATF standard, 1.4.3.3

T

The Offence of Bribery
Relevant Bribery Laws/Regulations, 7.1

Strict liability, 7.2
Extra territorial jurisdiction, 7.3
Penalty, 7.4

Terrorist Financing
Motivation, 1.3
Source of Funding, 1.3

www.ingramcontent.com/pod-product-compliance
Lightning Source LLC
Chambersburg PA
CBHW031325230926
51848CB00001B/90
* 9 7 8 9 7 8 2 7 8 7 9 0 3 *